maintance

THE WISDOM OF THE PSYCHE

D0826996

THE WISDOM
OF THE PSYCHE

Ann Belford Ulanov

COWLEY PUBLICATIONS
CAMBRIDGE, MASSACHUSETTS

© 1988 by Ann Belford Ulanov
All rights reserved.

Published in the United States of America
by Cowley Publications.
International Standard Book No.: 936384-61-1

Library of Congress Cataloging-In-Publication Data
Ulanov, Ann Belford.
    The wisdom of the psyche / Ann Belford Ulanov.
        p. cm.
    Includes bibliographies.
    ISBN 0-936384-61-1 : $8.95
        1. Religion and psychology. 2. Psychology, Religious. 3. Self. 4.
Good and evil. 5. Feminism—Religious aspects—Christianity.
I. Title.
BF51.U43 1988   88-15964
200'.1'9—dc19

COWLEY PUBLICATIONS
980 MEMORIAL DRIVE
CAMBRDIGE MA 02138

for

Barry

Acknowledgements

I would warmly like to acknowledge The Protestant Episcopal Seminary of Alexandria, Virginia and its President Richard Reid who invited me to give the Zabriskie Lectures in 1985. That community's lively response to the lectures encouraged me to develop them further into the present book.

My warm thanks go to Staley Hitchcock for his skill and helpfulness in typing the manuscript. And last, and first, and always, my gratitude to my husband, Barry Ulanov, to whom this book is dedicated.

ANN BELFORD ULANOV

TABLE OF CONTENTS

THE MINISTRY OF THE EGO

I.

We are accustomed in the Judeo-Christian tradition to believe that we should renounce the ego, sacrifice it, forsake it. Anything less is thought to be selfish, if not downright evil. What nonsense then—or worse, what blasphemy—to begin this book with the topic "The Ministry of the Ego"![1] I do so because of the precise ministry assigned the ego: to house what we have been given to be and to give it back to the giver.

What is the ego? It is the locus of the *I* we know ourselves to be. It is the carrier of consciousness in the personality. Part of the wisdom of the psyche moves us to grow a flexible and vigorous ego capable of housing all that belongs to us, capable of offering it to what is beyond ourselves. It is the ego, the sense of *I* that relates to the unconscious, rather than being swamped by it or splitting away from it. It is the ego, that sense of *I*, that meets other people's senses of *I*. It is the ego, that sense of *I*, that struggles toward God, that receives God, that prays to God. In this *I* resides the meeting points between conscious and unconscious, between self and other between soul and God. In psychoanalytic terms, The *I* is where we experience the true self, that sense we have of being alive and real and uniquely our own persons, in D. W. Winnicott's vocabulary. The *I* is the place of self, Heinz Kohut says, which is indefinable but essential, nuclear to the human personality. In Jung's language, the ego is the place where we meet the self, the center of the whole psyche.[2] Without the ego's response there is no connection; the self remains just a bunch of opposites. Great archetypal images wash in over consciousness and wash out again if there is no ego there to receive them, digest them, and channel them into life. We have the sad evidence of the toll an unreceived unconscious exacts from poor souls living ten, twenty, or thirty years in their pajamas in the back wards of mental hospitals. Confounded, sometimes assaulted, by fantastic images from the unconscious, lacking an ego in which to receive and house the images and live them, we lose both our center and our own sense of being an *I*. The ego is needed to reach that indefinable core that we call the soul life of a person.

Jacob Boehme's vision of the real objectively existing Christ in his soul came to him when he was eating off a pewter plate and saw reflected in the plate his own physical eye.[3] As it looked back at him, it was an image to him of the indwelling Christ beholding his soul. The indwelling Christ as the eye of God was looking at the eye of Jacob Boehme. God and the soul meet in this sense of I-ness. Thus does Yahweh reveal God—as an infinite, abundant, overflowing I-ness, saying to us, I am; I am who is with you; I am who is. And we need our own little finite, "I am" to answer back. This linking up of eye to eye is the basis of human community. Knowledge of this point of connection of the human and the divine is the specific resource Christians have to offer to our world where so many feel anxious and lost in large impersonal events, with no sense of I-ness, feeling they are merely negligible quantities in collective happenings. Recognition of the inestimable value of the person dwells at the heart of Judeo-

Christian faith. Each *I* reaches to that precious I-ness in other persons. We can see each other because God first sees us. *also catchy, does it flow from what has gone before?*

In and through and beyond the ego we consciously register the psyche's capacity to be related to the divine. It is a capacity we all share. It cuts across all our differences of class, economic status, educational level, color, sex, creed, historical era, nationality. We all possess this capacity to be aware of being related to something divine. And our psyche churns up images to speak of it.

One woman's dream makes this vividly clear.[4] She experienced it as a blessing. She felt it put her little *I* in touch with what is beyond herself. And not only what is beyond, but what is abundant, indeed what is joyous. She dreamt: "I'm standing in a museum looking at an abstract painting of bright colors—blue, yellow, and red bands of color in wavy lines move across the canvas. At the same time I look and see this painting, I hear it. The painting sings! Music comes forth from it. A big certitude wells up in me. This is it. This is it!"

That is a particular dream of a particular person. But we can all catch the sense of it, the bigness of it, its joyous quality. She felt linked up deep down inside her own sense of particular I-ness, to something of central importance, objectively there, far outside herself. Such dreams recall us to our own pivotal moments of linking up to what matters.

The ego is also the place where we register and suffer wounds, needs, problems, and struggle to solve them. We never do this in the abstract, but always in most particular and personal ways. Again, an example. A woman is gifted at connecting with others and seeing in each one their particular sense of I-ness. Indeed, she can feed it, and extend it, so that people like to be with her. They become more of themselves, nourished by her. They feel more possible. But she is aware that her sense of I-ness has a large hole in it. It's a hole she falls right into, where she feels not only inadequate but untenable as a person, a fake, without any sense of a coherent ego. She feels she is bad, all the more as she has painfully discovered that she has used her gifts to nourish others' sense of themselves to cover up this hole in her own ego. She had covered her own ego-lack by filling in someone else's. She had substituted making others feel alive and real when she herself had felt most fake and bad. In the midst of this, there came a lunch with a colleague, where she caught herself right in the act of pumping him up. She stopped. The conversation fell flat. She heard her own inner deadness, instead of the life and liveliness she was giving to him. She came out of herself in her despair of finding a self. She met her sense of lack and did not run away. In going into the *I* she felt was deficient, she began the journey beyond it. She stopped what looked like giving but was in fact taking, and started taking herself seriously. That was the beginning of real giving on her part—to herself, to others. Through such suffering, a central question is put to each of us. Do we listen to the *I* that we are? Do we house the bits of emptiness and despair that belong to us? Or do we use our ministry to others to cover them up and run away?

This, then, is the ministry of the ego: to claim the particular *I* given to us to live—to claim all of it, good, bad, fake, real—and to give it back to the giver. We have an ego in order to house what is given to us, to live it, to live it into life, and to offer it back to life's source. The ego is that small space, that small mite of consciousness, that precious bit without which we do not know that we are related to God. If we do not grasp the importance of the ego then its unlived life seeps unconsciously through all we do and we never get beyond it, to offer it to ourselves and to others. Too little awareness of the true claims of the ego produces too much of the inflated ego, with its possessiveness and its being possessed—by power, by need, by desirousness, by imitation, by what Augustine means by *cupiditas*.[5] Then, in Jung's language, we need the heavy hand of the self to crush the ego's boundless ambitions, a shock of fate to unseat it, even the threat of death to dispel the ego's illusion that it stands at the center of the universe.[6]

But we forget that the ego is also the portal for the larger self. The ego is the means by which the greater center comes into the world, the passageway through which the extraordinary comes through into the ordinary. Here this person and that one, in this small group of people struggling to worship, in that larger group trying to bring into the world the silent touch of grace it has felt, the ego acts as threshold for the move from center to world. As with people gathering at a concert who hear individual string voices playing together in a quartet, the whole is not the simple sum of the four parts, but a gathering of parts indispensable to the existence of the whole, all our separate egos together make perception of the whole beyond ourselves hearable, possible. We must always remember God does not want sacrifices, does not want egos served up as burnt offerings. What God asks is a living relationship, an "I am," an "I am who is," an "I am with you." What God wants is an answering "I am" too, one that says, "Here I am, too. I am with you."

The wisdom of the psyche is to produce an ego, a particular sense of *I* that will house and offer who we are. Here is the link to the church. It is as if the church were acting as the ego of the Christian world. I will put to the side, for the moment, all the obvious problems of the church which are not unlike the problems of ego identity—repressed bits, lost bits, outcast parts, splits, fragmentation, enfeeblements. I want to stress here, instead, that the church exists as a space of consciousness where people together, as a community, know themselves consciously in relation to God. Its ministry is precisely to share this consciousness, to reach to the outcast parts of the human family, to include the forgotten ones, those poor in spirit and sick in soul. The church is the place where people struggle together to open themselves to God, to recognize that we are all created by God for God, and to live in that society together. Like the ego in the psyche, that comes into being as the linking up of little sparks of light, little moments of consciousness that join together to make the light of a small ego, so the church is a place of flickering light in the darkness of our times, so fraught with fear, so anxious over all that troubles the world. The church in its scattered life across the globe shows, now here, now there, moments of real illumination as it links up to the central light of God. Our task is like that of the monasteries of old, to keep that flickering light alive in these dark ages.

Sociologically, the church acts as a buffer zone where opposites get housed, where the worst and the best of us as a human family can find a space to live. Surely, we all recognize that the church is the home of the lame, the halt, and the blind; not to mention the mediocre and the boring. Yet, this all too human church is also the place where the highest hopes of the human family, and the recognition of its deepest origins, not only occur, but persist—in memory, in celebration, in ritual. We live in the recognition that we are the ones, we in this world, in this flesh, for whom God has come. We see that we are created to praise God, to live in recognition of that God for whom we were made, summoned, saved.

The worst and the best of our energies come into this buffer zone of the church to find there a house in which to be sorted through, registered, linked up, differentiated. Here we can bring our failures, our lost hopes, our undared ambition, our refusal of what has been offered. Here we can find for them a shelter of mercy. Here we can bring our untamed wild energies that would blow up, root out, destroy, smash, blow away, shoot at, violate, and devour ourselves, one another, our world. The church is a zone of communication where the highest and the lowest, the best and the worst, can find a house in which to mix with each other, to intermingle, to be tamed and made into durable usable forms.

What sort of energies are these? I offer a concrete example. A woman dreams she is sought out by a younger woman for needed advice. She will see this younger woman in her office which, in the dream, opens onto a garden, so that what is outside can come inside. There is no barrier. Just as the younger woman arrives, the woman hears a snuffling, growling, snorting sound. And there, about to come into the office doors, is a great beast, a female beast, maybe with cub, like a wolverine or a wild boar or a bear. It is terrifying to her. End of dream.

The beast arrives with the younger woman but she knows nothing about it. That makes it all the more dangerous, because no one is conscious of it, let alone in control of it. The beast is free, then, to prowl into anyone's office, into anyone's life. It is that sort of energy we need to house in the spaces of our churches, whatever is howling and savage. Significantly, the dream links that untamed energy to the feminine, breaking into the meeting of two civilized women. The female animal may also be a mother animal, invading their space. It is as if the dream is saying that if this woman is to get the counsel she needs, there must be included with it the wild, untamed female energy as well as what we like to think of as ordered, civilized, refined. Church, like ego, must house it all. The church is a space where people struggle together with all forces, bestial included, and knowing the struggle will fail unless God shows mercy. The church is a place where every energy can be held and become transformed, made livable, made available, made fully accessible to the world. So the church, like the ego, performs a ministry of housing, a ministry of openness to what made us and still calls us its own. Insofar as the church does not bring this transcendent perspective to bear upon our world, all of it, and our personal issues, all of them, it fails in its mission.

What then of the clergy? You who care for the souls of your flock, who get up week after week and speak of the transcendent. You are training to go out into the world, and must strain daily to keep that flickering light alive so that the church may endure as house, as buffer zone, as agent of transformation. Who then are you? You are the housekeepers. You are like the widow looking for the lost mite, that missing bit so essential to the whole. You are like Martha making her house ready for her Lord. Or like Mary, listening to the Lord, taking everything deep down inside yourselves. You are like the ladies making sure there is enough oil to light the entry of the bridegroom, or like the woman who poured out all she had—her tears, her kisses, her hair—upon Jesus' feet. Or that other mysterious Mary who was the first to minister to Jesus on his way to the cross by anointing him with perfume and oil. You are like the Magdalene, the apostle to the apostles, announcing the resurrection. Like all housekeepers, you live and work in the trenches, not where life is lived as it should be, but where life is lived as in fact—flawed, frightening, harassing, painful. Housekeepers never live in a calm perfection, but always in the midst of dentists' appointments, meals to get, rooms to clean, accounts to settle, with broken people, people not awake, hungry people, people looking for and not finding one another. Housekeepers live in the midst of people trying wildly somehow to keep their lives together, to pay their taxes, get their children into school, get them through school, get them launched into their lives. People with broken relationships, people with good relationships, they all come, waiting, listening, wanting you, housekeepers of their souls, to tell them what has been said, to explain it. Will you tell us?

In the last decades of our century, this housekeeping task has become extremely hard. We live as if in the time of Jeremiah, who spoke of God being mad because so badly treated and ultimately deserted by Israel. We live in a time when many feel deserted by God, a time when people still can remember seeing their own children bashed in the head by Gestapo officers, and can see only too many events of the same kind still occurring when parents watch their children die without so much as a cold drink to give them, or a cool cloth to put on their burning foreheads. We live in a time where people are sent to Gulags, altogether deserted, not to be found again, many of them. We live in a time when strangers capture strangers on planes and keep them hot, exhausted, tired, dangerously ill, having to raise their hands to go to the bathroom. We live in a time when because people starve much food is gathered and sent to feed them and the food piles up on the docks because the regions that need the food are not of the political persuasion of the rulers of the

starving people. We live in a time where for many, countless numbers, the sense of I-ness is routinely trampled
upon. What terror, what misery! What a deprivation we
suffer in this loss of our hold on the center! Simple human
recognition becomes the priceless jewel for which the
world is held hostage. As in Jeremiah's time, grace is not
just lying around, ready at hand. We must look for it; we
must wait for it; we must long for it, And you,
housekeepers of the church, the housekeepers of the
space where the light may be seen flickering, and we with
you who try to reach to you and help prepare you for this
difficult job, all of us must be connecting links for the
many who wait, who long, who want to hear, who want
to come into our household.

This again is the ministry of the ego: so to house that
longing that it may be cried out not only in prayer but in
our movement through our daily life. This is the ministry
of the ego: to open to all parts of the psyche, and all the
kinds of *I* and I-nesses around the world, so that we may
become able to listen through our defenses of withdrawal
and attack, of denial and accusation, to hear that cry of
the heart which we can say, echoing Augustine, is God's
voice within us. Augustine is very clear about it: "Crying
to God is not done with the physical voice, but with the
heart; many are noisy with their mouths, but with their
hearts averted, and are able to obtain nothing. If, then,
you cry to God, cry out inwardly where God hears you."[7]
This is the ministry of the church, which in so many
ways acts like an ego for the community of Christians: to
remember together the cry from the heart, to confess
together our woundedness and to voice our hopes in
God's promise. Such community awareness points again
and again to God's presence in our midst. In the house of

the church we remember whom we belong to and who it is that calls us home.

II.

What might depth psychology contribute to this ministry? Depth psychology opens us up in new ways to the life of the psyche. It also opens up the life of the psyche to us in new ways—with all its struggles and yes, with its wisdom, too. Depth psychology calls us to be conscious, to stretch, to house in our egos all that is given us to be, our deepest longings, our fiercest dreads, the beliefs that inhabit us. Jose Ortega y Gasset describes belief as something we inhabit, something we stand upon.[8] It is not something we know about, but a comfortable ground that we simply take for granted. Depth psychology tells us that our unconscious feelings and images of God, our glimpses of the divine in our inner seeing and hearing and tasting and touch and smells are as vital to our religious life as are our conscious sincere professed beliefs. They comprise the substantial ground we stand upon, the belief we inhabit, where we live, from where we come.

Our unconscious images of God are rarely the same as our conscious professions of faith. A large gap exists between them and it is a major part of the ego's ministry to stretch enough to house this gap. Not knowing about the unconscious images of God we carry around does not make them go away, but rather quite the opposite. Like the woman with the beast, they come whether we know it or not, and all the more dangerously if we are unaware of them. These sorts of images or experiences—and we all have them—they are the ones we realize when we look back over our lives, that have deeply marked us. We may not understand them, but we never forget them. They can come in dreams; they can come in conversations; they can come in reading; they can come in public events; they can come in moments of intimacy, in moments of betrayal, in moments just before or after a death. They come in all sizes and shapes, and are very particular and peculiar to each of us.

There are extraordinary examples that make this point. Here is one. A man suffered all his life, as far as he could remember, all the way back into his childhood, from a sense of a threatening Void, a great emptiness that required a capital letter to express his experience, an emptiness that lurked always around the edges of all his significant experiences. In any moment of overwhelming intensity, in thought or feeling or sensation, he would feel himself go numb, as if paralyzed. And then, in this great sucking emptiness, everything he experienced vanished! He lost connection to all he had felt. For him it was a constant falling into an endless abyss. He was tortured by it. It made him lose all connection to his life, which he had gone on building despite this problem. He had married, achieved a profession, fathered children, and valued all highly. But in these moments of the Void, everything disappeared. He would lose all hope in what he was doing, all faith in his ability to do it. He suffered terribly and worked very hard to house this awful experience, to give it space, to make sense of it. He described it many times, many ways. He even dared, on occasion, imaginatively to go right into the Void and try to describe it from the inside. All this was his conscious work. The unconscious— I would say the wisdom of the psyche—rewarded him by giving an image in a dream of what was besetting him.

He dreamt that he was at his favorite place on earth, one where he had had an experience that marked him in the most positive way. It was a particular beach he liked where he always felt possible, valid, whole. He reported the dream: "As I stand on the beach along the river bed, on a bright clear summer day, the ocean surges mightily toward the beach and up the river, cutting away at the beach and gouging deeply into the channel of the river, going ever deeper. . . . As I look the water seems to go deeper and deeper, and then suddenly it is gone, absolutely gone, through a hole in the bedrock of the river channel! Within the now-empty river bed, there is a central pole around which six black men stand, depleted and still [he was white]. They are linked to the pole in some way. It has been their dancing which has caused the flooding of the ocean. When they stopped dancing, the waters subsided. Anonymous people around them think they ought to be reactivated. A feminine voice says, 'Something has gone wrong, something has gone awry. These men need relief, need rest.'" End of dream.

The dream scared the dreamer as much as the Void did. But see how the unconscious responds. It gives him another image. It is not just emptiness now. It is a matter of men enslaved, men having to dance, men needing rest. Their dancing or exhaustion clearly has to do with the intensity and flooding, or with the subsiding and emptiness. This image put the Void in a very different light for the dreamer. The problem is no longer one of emptiness but one of rhythm, finding the right flow from flooding to drying up. Further, the dream image stirred compassion in the dreamer for the plight of the six men, victimized men, driven like slaves. Their enslavement and their blackness connected to his victimization and his whiteness and suggested another way to look at his feel-

ing of being oppressed by the Void. Power and domina-
tion forced these men to translate into dance movement
the flooding and ebbing of tides. A great repression—
enslavement, really—of his own power to relate to the unconscious was suggested in this image, as well as a
hidden prejudice against the unconscious or fear of it or
wish to control it, maybe even to enslave it. Then suddenly comes the feminine voice to open up an entirely new
possibility. A better relation between black and white is
hinted as possible. The wisdom of the psyche is to hand
to this dreamer new images for his old problem, to house,
and then consider and work over to discover where he is,
who he is. Thus did the psyche set him his task for the
next several years: how to work on this, how to relieve
not just himself now, but these inner brothers who were
somehow victimized even more than himself; how to ex-
plore the new possibility the feminine voice announces.

In examples of this kind, we should think to bring their
materials into our own house of consciousness, to recall
experiences which have marked us, summoned us,
wounded us. For those experiences can be positive or
negative, like a grievous death or twisting perjury. But
the images, pictures of life's profoundest moments that
we inhabit and that we all carry around inside us, form
and reform our beliefs about God, God as connected to
us, God as distant from us.

It is the ego, the *I* in us that experiences these moments
and which must house them, even though a great gap
looms between them and our professed religious faith.
The ego is the linking place where we receive the wisdom
that comes from the psyche and the good news that comes
from the gospel.

From a theological point of view, as such examples sug-
gest, depth psychology adds a new line of hermeneutic

to religious studies. It doesn't replace other interpretive devices, but adds to them. We must ask about the psychological meaning of images in Scripture and tradition and bring into focus, next to them, the psychological meaning of unconscious images of God. For no religious education takes place which does not also address these private, personal images of God, these *pet* images of God, that the unconscious gives us.[9] No theological understanding really occurs if we leave out our personal and group pictures of God and their relation to the God we know from Scripture and tradition. No ethical discernment of principles of right action can be advanced without our acknowledging our images of inner enslavement and the drive to perfection that the psyche expresses in our compulsions, addictions, and acts of sabotage. No preaching reaches to the heart if it ignores the unconscious wishes, needs and fears of the congregation. And surely no spiritual counsel or direction proves effective that omits the spirit inhabiting the psyche. For the psyche is the flesh in which God comes to us. How can we then not house all that the psyche brings us?

If we fail to do so, it is not just a personal loss; it is a danger to our society. For these images, these experiences, and the woundings they bring us do not go away if we neglect them; they go unconscious. They live on in us, unhoused, free to accumulate more and more energy and to break out in violence, sometimes through the weakest links in our community. A person whose hold on consciousness is feeble can be contaminated by a group's unhoused psyche. Someone, for example, who is having fantasies of persecution may be pushed by group fantasies of persecution to pick up a gun and become the sniper who makes the headlines. He suddenly thinks perfect strangers are characters in a plot to kill him, and so he must shoot them first before they get him. Unconscious images can grow so strong they take over the ego entirely.

Unconscious images are unbelievably powerful. If we do not consciously stretch ourselves to give them room in us, they can fall onto the causes we take up, the values we serve, the movements we join, the theories we hold, inflating them, ultimately making them cruelly destructive.

From a theological point of view, we know all about this. This is what, in its worst phase, we call idolatry. Why does it happen? Because, to look at it from a psychological point of view, we fail to house what lives in us, and know that it is from us and bespeaks our longing for the ultimate, not the destructive element, now, but being itself. As a result of our failure to deal with them, these inner images become outer realities. Our private longings to have God to come clearly, certainly, into the midst of our life, of our race, of our sexuality, our politics and culture, of our faith, turn round on themselves. As a public force we use them to coerce our neighbor. We demand that our neighbor house what we cannot or will not allow to live in us.

Have we not seen God in the last decades named and renamed according to our private god-images—God as black, as female, as gay, as terrorist, as Marxist, as psychic force? Have we not seen our causes for justice, for peace, for conservation of the earth, become agents of bullying and guilt-making against those who do not agree? Even theology, dedicated to understanding systematically the reality of the Holy, can be put to sadistic use as a weapon of humiliation and tyranny. Even psychology, dedicated to hearing and seeing the specific I-ness of people, can become a weapon of contempt, making people feel small

and inferior for not fitting into the right developmental
stage on their way to health. Even our political causes,
which we hope and pray will improve the world, can become sadistic weapons to coerce others' agreement.

Theologically this is nothing new. Sin exists. No human
endeavor, no human value is immune to its invasion.
Temptations to idolatry abound in our world. But depth
psychology can help us here. It insists that we heed the
images of God that live within us. If we do not, it warns
us, those images will flood the world and contaminate
others instead of giving them hope. They will become the
idols we force on our neighbor. We disregard the psyche
at the risk of the whole faith drying up, as we can see in
the faltering life of so many contemporary churches. We
can see in the vacuum of a psyche-disregarding religion
the rush of the certainties of right and left to fill the void:
if only we would believe in this and this, only follow
these rules, all would be well. But programs and rules
cannot cover the gap left by the unhoused and untended
psyche. We must struggle to house in ourselves all the
ways in which God touches us, everywhere God reaches
us in our flesh, the flesh of our experiences, of our needs,
of our wounds. The man who suffered the sense of the
Void could not just paste the good news of the gospel over
that vortex. He had to grow his way down to the good
news, where it awaited him. The woman with the painting that sang to her ears had to lay that image of blessedness alongside the promise of God's blessing and see how
they grew together. She dared not substitute one for the
other.

Depth psychologists talk about such images and their
projections as ways we cover what happens to us, rescu-
ing our experiences, gathering them into nets of meaning.
This is how we build ground under us, from below, sup-

porting ourselves so we do not feel we are just hapless
victims of random events. If we do not house these images, we are left ungrounded in the flesh of the psyche.
And insofar as the church does not house this all-too-
human psyche, in each person, in the collective person, it
too risks being ungrounded, being irrelevant, not touching us where we live. Indeed, the whole ship threatens to
lose its mooring and go out to sea, leaving us stranded.

III.

But what of the other side? Depth psychology again and
again comes to a stop at its own borders. It is able only
then to point beyond itself. It can tell us a great deal about
how these images live in us, embody our longings, and
how our pictures of God function for our health or illness.
But surely we want more than this. We want to know if
they are real. We want to know not just how our images
of God function psychologically for health or illness in
us, but how they are true. In the jargon of psychoanalysis,
we want to know if this self-object, this image we have of
God, exists objectively.[10] We want to know if our God-
image speaks of God as well as ourselves. We want to see,
hear, touch, penetrate, receive that Other, that holy Other,
who lives objectively as an independent subject, standing
over against us, reaching out to us. We want to know who
breaks in, who is the One that comes to us, who changes
our whole way of perceiving the gap between us and the
divine by crossing over to us from the other side.

Here depth psychology's ministry stops. Its ministry
has been achieved if it unshackles us, opens us to the
housing of the ego, the receiving into consciousness of all
of which the psyche would speak, left to us now to be

sorted through and offered into life. It is only religion, theology, the church's life that dares to go beyond this boundary-line of depth psychology, to brave the unknown waters, to cross beyond the known into the unknown. The psyche's life is crucial, is fundamental to anything and everything we do. It cannot be ignored or hopped over. Neither can it be or give us all. It leads us where we must go, into the soul's life and stops. We are deposited there at that core of audacity and suppleness, that yearning and daring for what is beyond, while we are still in the flesh of the here and the now. The soul now dares to speak of this other in its own life so different from our life. For what really is the doctrine of the Trinity but an incomparably bold description of what God is doing when God isn't doing anything, when God is just sitting around, being? The soul's life is to seek to live with God. The soul does not concern itself unduly with how it is *experiencing* God, but rather concerns itself with how it is experiencing *God*. The difference of emphasis is enormous. The soul's life, after all, has to do with joy, the joyous shock of difference, the difference of the Other who comes through, who calls out, who pushes, punches, pounds, and addresses us, saying, "Here is what I have for you. Take it."

The gospel confronts us from this other side, telling us we never get to God from our side. God comes to us, breaks through to us—down and down, up and up, through successive layers, reaching right into our clearest and muddiest images, all our images, of God. We know, or think we know, that we do not get to God from our side anymore. Grown up, we think we have outgrown the images of God as a Santa Claus and ourselves as good little girls and boys doing the right thing. But do we really know that? Have we not just traded that childish god-im-

agery for another that is only superficially more sophisticated? Do we not think that if we could bring our plan
for justice to the earth, that would bring God's peace? Or
if we could bring our curriculum plan to our school, that
would be *the* significant theological answer? Or in
psychotherapy by working hard on dreams, and untan-
gling knots of neurosis, that surely we will bring ourselves closer to God? Or in the dangerous and touching
moment we find ourselves in history, under threat of
nuclear destruction, that our work in the antinuclear
cause is really doing God's work? Are not these all merely our ways of getting God to come to us and getting ourselves to God?

This is why the ministry of the ego is so important: It
makes us conscious of all these little gods and goddesses
that live in us, that we house within us. These are the ones
we bring to our endless offertories. The ego is the place
where we can become conscious of those authority
figures of super ego and ego ideal—values, causes, movements—with which we must make peace, which we must
even love in order to feel safe and secure.[11] Our very best
values and causes are still only ours. We need to know we
make them into gods and goddesses to give them some
shining importance. But God breaks through from the
other side, saying to us, "No, no. Come as you are now,
unfinished, not safe, not secure, not shining, not cured of
your neurosis, not finished with your dreams, even
without having brought your curriculum or your antinuclear program to fruition. Come before your cause has
taken effect, before your side has won. Come as you are,
inept, sinful, incomplete."

The Holy Spirit breaks through even into these secret
places, these cherished values, these wild dreams of con-
quest of all human problems. The spiritual life is not a

gloss on the surface, but something that digs down deep, right to our center, into the unconscious psyche, causing upheaval, pain, anxiety, touching our need to please, to be approved of, to be successful, touching our drive to perfect ourselves, bringing us finally then to the borders of despair. We despair because we can never make things right, never achieve perfection, never remake the world. Least of all can we earn our way to God. The Holy Spirit is always a surprise, and not always a gentle one.

One last example. A woman in one arduous period of her life was in despair over her relationships with men. They never worked out no matter what she did or what she didn't do. And she was sick of it. During that time she prayed the Jesus prayer, repeatedly. She said, "What happened was that something came into my heart and burnt it out! Jesus came in like fire, and a lot of stuff came up in me that was overwhelming. I had been seeing again and again all the ways in which I felt myself mistreated by men. And now I saw that I did not really see men at all. They were mere objects to me—to love me, to reassure me, to make me feel safe. The whole thing was reversed, upside down. It was like a revelation." Seeing that, she was freer to seek relationship with a man.

If grace works in us, things are turned upside down. We are brought to see our poverty, our utter dependence on divine creation to sustain us. Without it, we are nothing. We must know that. We are punched and pounded like bread dough until all the hot air is pushed out of us. We are brought to see at the center of our conscious being that there is one God. And that to this one God we bring all our gods and goddesses, all the little lights, all the values, all the problems, offering them to their author, offering them back to their giver. We are brought to obedience to this source of life in the midst of our lives.

There, in all our dependence and woundedness, the surprise comes. We know that our images for God, so full of our yearning and crafting, are not God, but that they may be that in us which knows God. We are found there, taken as we are, the gap crossed in one stride by God's love.

Here is the great calling and task of the clergy. You who keep the flock and tend the souls, you stand right there in the gap between all our human effort toward the good and the coming of God from the other side that both nullifies and accepts all our efforts. You stand right there in the gap between our images of God and God's self-presentation that always surprises us, woos us, wounds us, blesses us. You, our housekeepers, make space for all our images and all our projections, right alongside God's images for us, what tradition, Scripture, and doctrine tell us. You are the connecting link for the woman with the beast, the man struggling with the Void, the woman with the singing painting. How shall the psyche's wisdom grow together with the wisdom-giving God? How shall that gap ever be crossed? And what are the first things to fall into that gap? That is what the next chapters will address because the first things to be lost in religious life are always those two great daimons of the psyche—aggression and sex. Depth psychology researches and works intimately with those two mighty psychic forces that so beleaguer our world as they come to us in their projected forms. The next chapter will take up the psychological issue of aggression with its attendant theological issue of evil. The third will address sexuality, particularly the lost and neglected feminine that so often falls into the gap, that we are struggling so hard now to recover and receive.

Let us recognize here, with an appropriately solemn finality, that the ministry of the ego and the ministry of the church is to claim and to accept all that we are given to live and to offer it all back to the giver. Jung puts it nicely: "Each person has something specific to accept. . . . Let us just say that the thing we have to accept is whatever we want to escape."[12]

"Wisdom begins when we take things as they are. . . . Only by agreeing with facts as they are can we live on earth in our bodies.[13]

"It is tremendously important that people should be able to accept themselves. Otherwise the will of God cannot be lived."[14]

NOTES

1. This book is based on the Zabriskie Lectures I gave at Virginia Theological Seminary, Alexandria, Virginia, in October 1985.
2. It is interesting to note that theorists of quite different theoretical orientations converge in their descriptions of this mysterious and essential I-ness. See D. W. Winnicott, "Ego-Distortions in Terms of True and False Self," in *The Maturational Processes and the Facilitating Environment* (New York: International Universities Press, 1965): "At the earliest stage the True Self is the theoretical position from which come the spontaneous gesture and the personal idea. The spontaneous gesture is the True Self in action. Only the True Self can be creative and only the True Self can feel real . . ." (p. 148)

   "The True Self comes from the aliveness of the body tissues and the working of body-functions, including the heart's action and breathing. . . . There is but little point in formulating a True Self idea except for the

purpose of trying to understand the False Self, because it does no more than collect together the details
of the experience of aliveness." (p. 148)

See also Heinz Kohut, *How Does Analysis Cure?*, ed.
Arnold Goldberg, with the collaboration of Paul E.
Stepansky (Chicago: Chicago University Press, 1984):
"There is not one kind of healthy self—there are many
kinds." (p. 44) "The structure of the self . . . is the
theoretical correlate of those attributes of the self
which, in their sum total, define this actual concept of
self psychology. While the notion of psychic structure
is, like all theoretical constructions, no more than a
tautology, it is still an invaluable aid to our thought
and an indispensable tool when we communicate with
one another. It allows us to speak of the attributes of
the self in general terms, without specifying whether
we have in mind its cohesion, its strength, or its har-
mony—that is, without specifying whether we refer to
a person's experience of being whole and continuous,
of being fully alive and vigorous, or of being balanced
and organized. . . . And it allows us to evoke, again
without being specific, such diverse yet defining attributes of the self as those given by our abiding experience of being a center of initiative, of being a
recipient of impressions, of having cohesion in space
and continuity in time, and the like." (p. 99)

See also C. G. Jung, *Mysterium Coniunctionis*, *Collected Works*, Vol. 14, trans. R. F. C. Hull (New York:
Pantheon, 1963): ". . . our consciousness issues from a
dark body, the ego, which is the indispensable condition for all consciousness, the latter being nothing but
the association of an object or a content with the ego.
. . . One could define it as a *relatively constant per-
sonification of the unconscious itself*, or as the Schopen-

haurian mirror in which the unconscious becomes aware of its own face." (p. 107, par, 129) "Even a life dedicated to God is still lived by an ego, which speaks of an ego and asserts an ego in God's despite, which does not instantly merge itself with God but reserves for itself a freedom and a will which it sets up outside God and against him." (p. 170, par. 206) ". . . the psychological recognition that God cannot be experienced at all unless this futile and ridiculous ego offers a modest vessel in which to catch the effluence of the Most High and name it with his name." (p. 215, par. 284)

3. See Jacob Boehme, *The Way to Christ*, trans. Peter Erb (New York: Paulist Press, 1978), p. 6.

4. All examples are taken from my practice as a psychoanalyst unless otherwise noted, with thanks to the persons who gave me permission to use their material.

The reader will note my debt to Jung who, in contrast to Freud, took seriously the "manifest dream," that is, the dream story as we remember it upon awakening: "dreams . . . are facts from which we must proceed." Freud exercised his "interpretation of suspicion" (as Ricoeur called it) against the dream text, understanding it as a disguise constructed by means of condensation, displacement, censorship, symbolism and secondary elaboration to hide the latent and real meaning of the dream. This latent dream wish is made respectable by such "dream work" so that it can pass into consciousness. Interpreting a dream, we unravel and discard the wrapping of the dream text in order to uncover the real wish hidden within it.

Jung begins from a completely different departure point. For him the dream walks in like an animal. We

must meet it on its terms and not be too quick to translate it and accommodate it in our terms of a concep-
tual consciousness. The unconscious presents us with
a dream picture that compensates for our conscious
view by presenting an omitted factor or an additional
point of view. Jung has complex methods of interpreting the dream text that include what he calls taking up
the context, directed association, archetypal
amplification, but he insists we must greet each dream
anew, knowing more and more about what it means
until we can enter into conversation with it. The attitude of respect for the otherness of our dreams lasts
and grows. It proves useful to every dreamer, whether
or not in analysis. It opens us to the other point of view
represented by the unconscious residing objectively
within our subjectivity.

Other psychoanalysts seem to be returning to this
view. Masud Khan, for example, writes about the
value of the experience of dreaming in contrast to the
remembered dream text. The dream text, I would add,
can come to be so separated from ordinary human experience for us that we may come to confine the examination of the meaning of our dreams to the
analytic consulting room, putting it beyond our reach
unless we have an analyst to decipher its meanings for
us. On the analyst's side, such confinement encourages something like fetishism about the dream
text, an approach that altogether overlooks the fact
that it is the dreaming of the dream that works its healing effects upon the dreamer. Ideally, and with luck,
we can experience the value both of the dreaming experience and the interpretation of the dream-text.

I do not give a complete interpretation of the
dreams cited here. To do so would involve a case

presentation in detail that would violate the dreamer's confidentiality.

See S. Freud, *On Dreams*, trans. James Strachey (New York: Norton, 1952); see also S. Freud, *New Introductory Lectures of Psychoanalysis*, trans. James Strachey, lecture XXIX, "Revision of the Theory of Dreams," lecture XXX, "Dreams and Occultism" (New York: Norton, 1965); see C. G. Jung, *Memories, Dreams, Reflections*, ed. Aniela Jaffé, trans. Richard and Clara Winston (New York: Pantheon, 1963), p. 171, See also C. G. Jung, "General Aspects of Dream Psychology" and "On the Nature of Dreams" in *The Structure and Dynamics of the Psyche, Collected Works*, Vol. 8, trans. R. F. C. Hull (New York: Pantheon, 1960); see also Prince M. Masud R. Khan, "Beyond the Dreaming Experience" in *Hidden Selves Between Theory and Practice in Psychoanalysis* (New York: International Universities Press, 1983).

5. Augustine defines cupidity in contrast to charity: "I call 'charity' the motion of the soul toward the enjoyment of God for His own sake, and the enjoyment of one's self and of one's neighbor for the sake of God: but 'cupidity' is a motion of the soul toward the enjoyment of one's self, one's neighbor, or any corporal thing for the sake of something other than God. That which uncontrolled cupidity does to corrupt the soul and its body is called a 'vice'; what it does in such a way that someone else is harmed is called a 'crime.' And these are the two classes of all sins, but vices occur first. When vices have emptied the soul and led it to a kind of extreme hunger, it leaps into crimes by means of which impediments to the vices may be removed or the vices themselves sustained. On the other hand, what charity does to the charitable person is

called 'utility'; what it does to benefit one's neighbor
is called 'beneficence.' And here utility occurs first, for
no one may benefit another with that which he does
not have himself. The more the reign of cupidity is de-
stroyed, the more charity is increased." St. Augustine,
On Christian Doctrine, trans. D. W. Robertson, Jr. (New
York: Bobbs-Merrill, 1958), pp. 88–89.

6. The off-quoted sentence of Jung's, "the experience of
the self is always a defeat for the ego," describes an ac-
curate state of affairs if the ego is disordered by inflation. This notion of our experiences of the self as being
opposed to our ego-needs and ambitions also touches
on the troubling mystery of what Jung called the dark
side of God. Even if the implied ontology is suspect,
we all know something about experiences of undeserved but unavoidable suffering and injustice. Our
fate seems to us jinxed or crossed by a dark shadow.
Terrible things befall us and wrench anguished questions from us about the nature of God's goodness or
even the value of existence itself. How can there be a
God if the suffering in the Holocaust or the bombing
of Hiroshima can happen? How can God allow a child
to die a long, slow death from famine or from a painful wasting disease?

Jung asks such questions and struggles toward an
answer by locating evil in God, evil that he defines as
God's unconsciousness. Even, as I said above, if we
find Jung's speculative ontology suspect, the vigor
and passion of his questioning call us to reflect on such
experiences, on events that oppose everything our
egos, both individually and collectively, stand for.
Such experiences do darken us. We often cannot see
our way through them. We suffer. We can only see then
that God's ways are not our ways. Such experiences

strongly move us, if they do not actually force us to change our ways and our ways of understanding ourselves and God. Otherwise we are not easily able to survive such experiences. See C. G. Jung, *Mysterium Coniunctionis, Collected Works*, Vol. 14, p. 546, par. 778.

7. On Psalm 30:3–10; cited in Thomas A. Hand, O.S.A., *Saint Augustine On Prayer* (Westminster: Newman Press, 1963), p. 70.

8. Jose Ortega y Gasset, *Historical Reason* (New York: Norton, 1984): ". . . we have *ideas*, but we inhabit *beliefs*. Man always lives in the belief of *this* or *that*, and on the basis of these beliefs—which to him are reality itself—he exists, behaves and thinks. Thus even the most skeptical of man is a believer, and profoundly credulous.

"It surprises me that Christian theologians never thought of this notion of belief, which would have enabled them to arrive at a simpler, more solid concept of faith, and to have provided—for the first time, albeit in a one sided way—a concrete, controllable meaning for St. Paul's sublime phrase that "we move, live, and are" in Christ." (p. 21)

9. Ana-Marie Rizzuto, *The Hands of the Living God* (Chicago: University of Chicago Press, 1979). Rizzuto traces the development of our "representations" for God but expressly eschews the question whether or not they are true. She traces the roots of such God-representations in our psychic history and examines the kind of image it produces, but does not ask whether it points to something that exists. This is an ego-question, she says, this asking about the reality of God. She is concerned instead with the unconscious image for God (see pp. 4, 36, 48, 211).

10. The term "selfobject" coined by Heinz Kohut and a

synonomous term, "subjective object," coined by D. W. Winnicott, refer to our human capacity and need to relate to others only in terms of how they reflect or mirror ourselves, our needs, our wishes, our own potentialities. We are also capable of relating to others as "objective objects," as others existing in their own subjectivity over against us or at least distinct from us. In that way, others become objective objects. Kohut's work on narcissism explores in detail three major ways we relate to others as selfobjects. We need others to mirror our nuclear (but still grandiose) self; we need to idealize others and (temporarily) merge with them; we need to see others as a sort of twin or alter ego who shares with us a basic likeness, a sameness really, and thus reinforces us. Kohut says we need self-objects our whole life long, though the way we relate to them becomes, with luck and with maturity, less archaic. He implies that a mature person would relate to others in two ways, both as a selfobject and an objective object.

Winnicott describes the transition from seeing others as selfobjects to seeing them as objective persons in their own right as dependent on aggression. We are frustrated when an object turns out not to be under our subjective control! We get mad. We are not omnipotent. But if the object survives our attack and the destruction of what we wish it to be (our projection), we discover the existence of the object in its own right, as quite other than ourselves. See Heinz Kohut, *How Does Analysis Cure?*, chapter 4; see also D. W. Winnicott, *Playing and Reality* (London: Tavistock), chapter 6.

These theories bear directly on our images of God. Is God more than a wish-God? Does God exist as the transcendent other for us? How much do we pray to God as a mirror for our group or individual needs and how much do we see God as other than our projections? Jung takes up these questions more than other depth psychologists when he asks so directly whether our God-images point to a real existing deity.

For discussions of these theories in relation to religious belief, see Ann Belford Ulanov, "What Do We Think People Are Doing When They Pray?" in *Picturing God* (Cambridge, MA: Cowley Publications, 1986). See also Ann and Barry Ulanov, *Religion and the Unconscious* (Philadelphia: Westminster Press, 1975), pp. 39–42.

11. The Cistercian Abbot André Louf writes of the monk's task of coming to terms not only with his outer ideals but also with an ego-ideal within himself. All "striving for perfection does not in any way correspond to the Gospel." True humility means liberation from even such good ideals. "It is God who calls a man and then gives him grace. If we want to do it under our own steam then nothing can come of it." André Louf, "Humility and Obedience in Monastic Initiation," *Cistercian Studies*, Vol. XVIII, 1983:4, p. 266.

12. C. G. Jung, *The Visions Seminars*, 2 vols. (Zurich: Spring Publications, 1976), Vol. 2, p. 321.

13. Ibid., Vol. 1, p. 203.

14. Ibid., Vol. 1, p. 135.

THE DEVIL'S TRICK

I.

The Devil is an enduring image in our culture, an archetypal one that gives us a way to talk about the reality of evil that we all experience. We know evil directly. We know it as a threat that comes to us in subtle tempting ways, the ways of the Devil. The Devil is a trickster, renowned for his dazzling light-bringing nature, not trying Jesus, for example, with cheap and trivial temptations in the wilderness. He tempts Jesus with the greatest of human hopes: to feed the starving; with the ability to give food to poor persons afflicted by famine; with the resource to give food to a mind, so that children will not be passed from class to class to graduation without learning how to read or write or think; with food for the imagination, so that people will not be left starved in their spirits. The Devil comes with a lustrous proposition: Bring peace to our world; bring us a united and just government. How much we need that, with the strife in Central America, the strife in South Africa, the strife in Lebanon, Iran, Iraq, everywhere! The Devil comes with the most pressing of temptations: show us your God; show us with irrefutable proof that you are God; show us a god we can all recognize and honor, and so be loosed from the religious fanaticisms that align themselves with terrorism.

The Devil is a trickster, the greatest of the sons of light, confronting Jesus with our most heart-felt needs and

highest values. How can we resist? Only the most hard-
hearted of us could hold out for the sake of a principle in
the face of so much human need and longing. The Devil
is also a liar and a cheat and a dullard. His light dazzles
but does not glow, it scintillates, but does not illuminate.
It reflects, but does not originate. He tempts us, and the
best among us, with pseudo-problems entirely cut away
from real mysteries. He yokes us with a false cross in
place of the real one. He captures us in just that gap discussed before—that gap between our images of God and
God's self-disclosure, that place of discrepancy between
the wisdom of the psyche and the wisdom of Scripture,
that space where the edges do not touch, the gap between
what we yearn toward as the ideal and what actually confronts us as reality. In that mysterious space we may fall,
and fall endlessly, as if into an abyss, fall as far as mad-
ness. If we can house that gap in consciousness, we may
come to fill it with imagination on the inside and full-
bodied living from the outside and thus receive the grace
to correspond with all that comes across from God's side.[1]
Jesus went before us into that wilderness of temptation
at the frontiers of evil. The Devil tempts us just as he
tempted Jesus, in beguiling voices that speak of our most
urgent needs for food, for nurture, for justice, for faith,
for hope.

The Devil always tempts us in large terms. Like the
Manicheans, he makes evil seem unmistakably alive to
us, big, strong, more powerful than the good. His voice
insinuates itself into the voices that attack the traditional
notion of evil as the privation of good, explaining that
that doctrine fails to give evil enough reality. We think of
the injustice in South Africa and the riotous killing in
reaction to it which only confounds the confusion. We
think of insidious threats of Alzheimer's Disease, where

people lose their minds in handfuls of meaning and memory; those who watch it, as one daughter wrote of her mother, see their loved ones going crazy right there before their eyes. We think of the persecution of the Jews in Soviet Russia. We think of the stealing of Tibet, a whole country, by Mao's China. We think of so many wrongs, so much violence and misery. We feel as if we are the hostages in a hijacked plane, held imprisoned by evil forces. Evil seems not just as strong and real and good, but much stronger, ready to overtake us completely.

The Devil's trick, expressed in grand terms, is to make us believe he has that much power, so we had better make a deal—and fast. The Devil's trick is to make us let go of the good to fight the evil, and even worse, to lead us to let go of an evil we can do something about to work for an abstract and idealized good that can never be realized.

The Devil's trick in small and personal terms effects the same kind of reversal. There are many examples. Here is one. A man dreams that he and a colleague are talking. The friend takes a strong line. He says that children must be brought up to know that homosexuality is an alternative life-style. The dreamer in the dream knows there is a trick here. It is all the more poignant that the dreamer knows this, because in his actual waking life he is wrestling with his own homosexuality. He knows in the dream that the trick is to make him fall for the either/or argument: he must take one or the other position, either to press for the alternative life-style position or to defy and refute it. Either way, he must get into the argument, take a side, pro or con. Instead, the dreamer (that is, the dream-ego) says in the dream: "That's not the issue. What matters is the relationship to the child. That's what counts." What the dream-ego is dealing with in that dream is not only a parent's relation to a child, but in our life as adults our relationship to the child within each of us.[2] The Devil's trick is to steer us off course into the turbulence of insoluble arguments. For even if we arrived at definitions, the actual situation of each individual parent-child couple, and of each individual person faced with interior struggles of this sort would prove an exception to the rule. The real issue is the quality of relationship and it is about that quality that the question must be asked, without any pretentious rhetoric about abstract positions.[3]

A second example: A woman in analysis had done long and good work. She came to a crisis in her life where everything changed: her profession, her personal relationships, her sense of herself, At the bottom of all of this change was the task of coming finally to recognize and take hold of her own particular value as a person and as a woman, a task which had always been left hidden in the shadows. In this period of the work, I myself became much more intense and spoke rather bluntly and urgently about the importance of taking her value seriously. She went home touched, and cried, cried a lot, she told me at the next session. What had made her cry was the sense that I had cared about her, not just as a patient but as a person, as a woman, as one woman to another. Which was true. I did, and I do. My caring carried extra weight because of her own lack of it and the neglect of others in her life that followed her poor sense of herself as a female and as a person. Then entered the Devil's trick. She did not want to lose this caring, and she did not want to lose knowing about this caring. So she went unconscious about it. To claim it, she hid it. To keep it alive, she buried it. To hold it, she let go of it. The trick she fell for was that consciousness of the relationship would destroy it and that unconsciousness of it would preserve it. That is the great lie. Not knowing about it is to lose it. To know and feel it is to have it. The Devil's trick is to let go of the good she found to protect against the evil of losing it. That is the Devil, in religious language, making one think something is nothing, and that nothing somehow preserves the something. The Devil's trick effects a privation of the woman's own concrete being in this case, while promising protection for that very being. It is the anti-ego trick, persuading us, individually or collectively, that we are not what we think we are and should not even consider the possibility that we see ourselves correctly when we see ourselves as having substance.

Another significant example concerns those primordial experiences I spoke of in the first lecture.[4] Whether in dream, fantasy, or encounter with others, in the world of nature or in a world event, something marks us, strikes into us, helping to make up and define our relation to the infinite. From such experiences we gain images that help construct truth as we have come to know it and be known by it. The trick of the Devil is to lure us into perjuring that truth. Those events that mark us, that we may not understand, but that we never forget, form and reform our images of God, our images of self. The trick of the Devil is to make us act as if those events never happened. To turn our backs on them. This is the Devil's pact. We sign it when we say to ourselves, "I will give this up in exchange for safety, success, power."

In psychoanalytic terms, such action is collusion with what attacks and vitiates our will to live. We then feel confusion, chronic self-doubt, and a total emptying. We just blank out. We forget what we know. We fade, as if invisible to what we are doing, yet a still small voice also knows what we are doing. But then we cover over that voice with lies or with indulgent bouts of guilt, self-

recrimination, and self-repudiation which carefully
avoid the particular spot where we turned away from the
good. We leave something homeless that should be
housed. We let go of the good as it was when it walked
into our lives.

Psychologically we deal with this act of spiritual perjury by spurious defenses whose rigidities work as much
harm as they do protective comfort. We split into opposites, hoarding the good but not spending it by living
it, and projecting all the bad on our neighbors. Or we hide
the good kernel to preserve it and thereby seal it up in its
original infantile state where it is unable to mature
through contact with reality. Melanie Klein suggests that
that is the situation of criminals.[5] To them the good seems
so fragile and the bad so robust, that to keep the good
alive they hide it in the unconscious and live off the bad,
committing crimes to live out their guilt over the bad and
over not living the good that belongs to them.

Theologically, such acts of collusion lead to a false
cross. This fascinating image reminds us that the lie that
is closest to the truth is always the most dangerous. Is not
Lucifer the brightest of the angels? The false cross brings
real suffering, but the suffering goes nowhere. The false
cross attaches itself to a surrogate problem that we think
must be solved, away from the mystery that we must live
with.

The real cross leads to suffering that opens to remorse,
reparation, resurrection. The false cross presents very different results as the following example indicates. A
woman sought analysis, saying she felt very guilty over
what she felt was promiscuous sexual behavior. After a
good deal of listening and sorting through, it turned out
her guilt was misplaced. In all her experience, she had
never been touched, had never been opened to her own

feelings or to another person and had herself never opened to another whom she clearly experienced as an "other." The real cross was this tightly closed feeling, of being firmly shut up, not unlike what Kierkegaard talks about.[6] The false cross, the pseudo-problem, was a question for her. What is the matter with my sexuality? What has happened to it? Where is it? One could spend years of work on this false issue, colluding with it, never getting to the real task. Indeed, what the woman referred to as her promiscuous behavior could also be understood as a desperate search for human contact.

In another example, a mother worried about her grown-up daughter. The daughter in her younger life had suffered a very serious depression. That had to do with bad parenting on both the mother's and father's part. The mother and the father and the daughter had worked very hard together, and separately, to repair their relationship, to make amends, to make restitution for pain and wounds they had inflicted and to build a new and healthy relationship. They succeeded. A great deal changed in both the daughter's and the parents' lives. Now, some years later, the daughter again falls into a depression. The mother feels rising in her the old guilt—what she did not give, or do, and what she did do wrongly. The pseudo-problem, the false cross in this situation, is the mother falling into well-worn ruts of guilt and becoming obsessively absorbed in her daughter's problems. The real cross for the mother is to let her daughter go into her own life, which means even allowing room for her own depressions, for her own reasons, not simply those her mother caused. The false cross is the self-indulgent bout of guilt again, seemingly on the daughter's behalf, that puts the mother right at the center of her daughter's life while avoiding what faces her in her own life. The real cross is to realize, as all of us must do, that those children whom we love are different, separate beings, their own beings, finally. They, who are flesh of our flesh and bone of our bone, who as little ones carried our projections of our own truest self, who bring the future to us and promise to make us live on beyond our past, must grow up to be separate people whose otherness we must recognize and respect. They go off into their own lives and they must be allowed to go and to make their own mistakes, as well as their own successes. The mother in this example is tempted to make a problem out of a mystery. How can she make sure her daughter will not be depressed? The mother must face the mysterious pain of separation from her own child, as all of us who are parents must do with our children. The real cross is letting go, standing by if our child calls, but not pressing if the child does not call.

We can speculate that the false cross facing those of us who were teaching in the 1960's was to solve all our students' objections to the status quo by giving into their demands and threats. But the real cross was to face not the exaggerations and distortions but the kernel of truth in their plaints, namely that the soul had gone out of some teaching, that some teachers no longer were giving real food in their teaching, that passion had been replaced by pedantry. The real cross was to try to face the fact that students avoided learning by failing to bring their own passion to the subject-matter, that they turned away from the soul of their work by creating a rumpus, an ersatz student life filled with passion that quickly became violent in some places. The real cross means looking at our failures and being tough enough to bear the failures of others without turning cynical or, worse, simple-mindedly retaliatory or condoning. This suffering means the hard work of trying to repair the bridge of trust between student and teacher and between both of them and the truth lying hidden in the material they study. Suffering of this kind leads to a possible renaissance of learning that touches the heart as well as the head, and informs the mind as well as moving the emotions. The false cross way leads to the endless suffering of fruitless, sprawling committee meetings that spawn more committees that move relentlessly into new rules and regulations and farther and farther away from the fire of the teaching-learning ignition. In some schools all classes were cancelled so that people could attend committee meetings.

Still another example, though a more general one, concerns any of us when we find ourselves in insoluble situations at work where we are in someone else's power. Sometimes what happens is what in psychoanalysis we call a double bind—the infamous situation where whatever you do you are damned if you do and damned if you do not. Something is deeply wrong in the interaction. If you speak up, those in authority over you are going to be more annoyed with you, more punitive, more entirely negative. If you do not speak up, you feel like a coward and a dolt, betraying the truth. There is no way to win. The false cross is the real suffering as we go round and round in this squirrel cage, trying to fix a situation that cannot be fixed—attempting this, then that, then the other thing, all to no avail. The real cross is suffering the hard reality that sometimes situations are in fact insoluble. They cannot be fixed and nothing we come up with from our egos is going to get them right. A gap looms—between what should happen—mutual confession and reconciliation—and what does happen: impasse. All ego-efforts, from either side, fail. The real cross is suffering the death of one's ego in that situation, of insights that prove ineffective, of hopes that are dashed, of a carefully drawn plan which proves futile. One is stuck. The real cross is suffering the pain of being stuck, held fast in a life-killing situation, struggling to ask what the meaning is of being faced with such an impasse. That struggle opens up an abyss of evil beneath our feet, a widening gap that threatens our entire stance. How can we work in a situation where agreement cannot be reached, where reason does not prevail, where even if we see the solution, it does not come right but can only go wrong?

These questions reveal the issue of the real cross: Can we stay reaching toward the center even in a situation of seemingly unending conflict? Can we keep groping in the dark toward the center when we seem doomed to stay fixed in an insoluble argument or difficulty?

The real cross can lead to the psyche's recognition of a more mysterious source, a recognition that sets the whole problem in a new light. When we investigate the psychic dimensions of such conflict we usually discover the transference of past problems with loved parents into present difficulties with our employer or others in authority over us. The present conflict usually hides within itself an earlier wound. Thus reaching agreement in the present amounts to healing a bruise from the past. The present conflict draws fuel from past unhealed suffering. That is what makes the present impasse so dangerous. Not only do we face the grave, immediate consequences of failing to reach agreement, but we also risk the past opening up again to drag us back down into that cave of early suffering where we must submit again to rejection by a parent, transformed now into the figure of the misunderstanding and tyrannical boss.

Depth psychology helps sort out the past from the present, the transference from current relationships to past ones. That helps. Sometimes it even solves seemingly insoluble problems. More often, however, it unshackles us only to let us see the depth of insolubility, not only in the present problem but in the earlier problem as well. I am reminded of Freud's remark that freed from neurotic suffering we are able to face the real miseries of life, and Jung's comment that neurotic suffering is the price we pay for refusing to suffer legitimately. The point is that understanding the psychic complexities of transference does not spring us loose from the mystery of insoluble conflicts. In fact, the wisdom of the psyche only enforces more strongly and deeply the wisdom of the spirit that is tough enough to recognize that reason, good intention, and even sharp insight are no guarantee that we can whisk away intractable blockages that stand up against us, in our world, in ourselves.

The psalmist's cry, From whence cometh my help? and the answer, My help cometh from the Lord, lead to the mystery of answers that arise from insoluble problems in the form of quite different questions—How can we keep open to the center in such impossible situations? How can we go on yearning toward the other side when all roads are blocked from our side? How can we go on living humanely in such inhumane situations? What is the meaning of being stuck? What should I turn around to see?

Maybe it is to see another missing piece of my past, or a piece of another person's past that so determines his present. Maybe I am meant to see the finitude of all human solutions. Maybe I am brought to see that whatever grace breaks through the blockage always comes into the situation from a mysterious source that I

myself cannot devise nor take apart or explain even when
such action is urgently needed. Maybe that is the point:
to see the marvel of grace, that mysterious something that
rearranges the opposites of insoluble problems, thus unexpectedly changing everything, the past as well as the
future, by breaking in upon the present. The real cross
yields outcomes. The false cross does not.[7]

The Devil's trick of handing us a false cross is not
restricted to small-scale events. It often seeks out huge
theaters for its devastating performance. Here, the trick
is to make us let go of the evil in the small that we can do
something about, to come up with the utopian solution
in the large that we cannot ever actualize—the perfect
plan, the faultless formula, the finished new vision. I
think religious people are particularly susceptible to this
trick. Perhaps we are more sensitive to others pain? Perhaps we are more gullible, more prone to utopian solutions. We are easily lured from the small thing in place,
the minor evil we can do something about, toward the
great evil in the abstract, threatening the continent, the
globe, about which we can make portentous pronounce-
ments. We say to ourselves, and we preach to others (the
church has a lot to answer for here) that ours is a selfish,
parochial, narrow-visioned, self-indulgent, morbidly in-
trospective world, where we concentrate energy on the
small at the expense of the large. We fall into temptation
to be drawn from the concrete into the abstract, forgetting
that we get to the larger only through the smaller. Jesus
was born of Mary, not of womankind in general. God
came to us in Jesus, not in a group plan nor a political
party or a health program, reaching out to all of us
through one particular man. And so we are cured, one at
a time. Thus does community grow among us, soul by
soul, down into the roots of each of us.

This approach may seem overly modest, but it is God's approach and it works. We depend on each other, each particular other, to link up and keep the whole circle alive. In Springfield, Massachusetts there was a man a few years ago who decided to organize help for the retarded persons in his community. He did extraordinarily well. Because of his success a local radio station interviewed him. How did he do this? "Simple," he said. He went to different individuals to make his case and then word just got around of the possibility for each person, each family, each group of friends to make one retarded person in the community the most important person for them outside the immediate family or circle of friends. And then, suddenly, there was nobody left outside the circle. Everybody had somebody who thought he or she was the most important person. The interviewer enthusiastically said: Well, can't we make this bigger? Can't we make this into a program? Can't the country do this? The man said: No! No government, no program, no nothing. Just this way.[8] One linked up to one, linked up to one, linked up to one. The Devil's trick is to come in and break those links, to make us think that they are not worth much, that they are too slow and too modest a way to help. Maybe so, but they work and they last. People are changed, not just new programs mounted.

Whereas one version of the Devil's trick is to make us let go of the good in order to fight against evil, the other version is to make us let go of the evil we can do something about that is concrete, even if small, in the name of an abstract idealized good, How then do we trick the trickster? By admitting the evil that belongs to us and claiming the good given to us, however small.

II.

The Devil loves to trick us away from the real cross to the false one. He offers, with particular skill in the late twentieth century, in the time of existentialist rhetoric, the lure of nothingness, to make something into nothing and nothing into something. The woman who glowed with new consciousness of being valued for her self was tempted to make it nothing by not knowing about it, by not keeping it in consciousness. The dreamer was tempted to get stuck in arguing the case either for or against a position about homosexuality and losing sight of the real connection between parent and child. Jung attacked the Christian notion of evil as the privation of good as a making of nothing out of the something of evil. Evil is real, Jung argued, not a privation. He felt the traditional idea dangerously tempted us to deny the reality of our own shadows, and of evil itself.[9]

Jung fell for the Devil's trick, I think, and missed the sophisticated psychological description the *privatio boni* gives us of evil's reality. For what is evil after all, what is its reality? It is a real force of nothingness that pulls us away from the being that is there, available and accessible that we can claim as we swirl toward emptiness, disintegration, blockage, obstruction. Evil spins us away from the center, dissolving our perception of it, breaking into pieces our experience of it, luring us to place more and more parts in front of ourselves so that we can move away from being present and open to the real self we are given to be. We take being tired, being busy, being caught by our jobs as ways of keeping from contemplating the good that is there. We put second, third, eighth, fiftieth things first in place of putting first things first. Evil makes absence where there was presence, makes nothing where there was something. It spins us into the void, into disintegration, into envy and resentment. As Barth said, "When I speak of *das Nichtige*, I cannot mean that evil is nothing, that it does not exist, or that it has no reality.[10]

Evil is all too real a force, a driving force that precedes deprivation, a force that cuts things off at the roots so nothing can grow. So many events of our history and our present world make this all too clear in ways that break the heart. The terrible suffering comes to mind of those Japanese school girls who looking skyward into the amazing flash of the exploding atomic bomb had their eyelids permanently burnt off from its heat. Children can be born to parents who do not, or cannot, love them, who may torture them psychologically or physically, leaving them crippled for life. People can be born into a land of dust, knowing from the first breath of consciousness to the last moment before they die the assault of dirty air and sterile earth, of constant hunger for better things, ordinary better things. Worse still, such scarring, such torturing, such starving could be ameliorated, if not cured, but it is not because of red tape, political infighting, financial dealing, and all the small mean-spiritedness we inflict upon each other. Evil is the stopping up of love; the withholding of warm response; the petty malice that amasses more and more rage and hate, so that it breaks out in savage acts of rape and murder. Yes, evil is all too real; evil is that dark hole within us where we turn away from good and may fall into the abyss itself.

What Jung was after, I believe, is the psychological and religious truth that we must admit to ourselves, just how strong evil is. It is not something we can get around or ignore. What he missed, I believe, is the greater theological truth—that good is stronger than evil and of a different order of being. Created being is good. The being we are

given is held in the circle of relationship of Creator and
creature. Evil is the force that makes us deny that relationship and seek to break it. Claiming both kinds of truth,
psychological and theological, we do not fall for the
Devil's trick. We trick the trickster by knowing just how
powerful evil is, and also knowing that it is not as powerful as good, not of the same order of being. The Devil's
trick is out-tricked by our effort to claim the evil that
vitiates us individually and communally, that would
make nothing of the good given us, that would destroy
our vision of the good, and turn us away from the radiat-
ing presence of good to the absenting forces of evil.

Take this example of a woman's dream that gave her
an unforgettable image of what assaulted her in her life
as evil. "A huge dog jumps up on me and puts its enormous paws around my face. It wraps its front legs around
me, and it goes for me. Finally, it puts its great teeth
around my eyes. I wake up in terror." She falls right back
to sleep and dreams again, this time, she feels, of what to
her is an image and vision of the good. "God comes down;
God comes down a staircase in a house. It has been a long
time since we've seen her. God is a she. Yet, when she gets
downstairs to where we live, she is not God but rather the
one who loves God. She is ordinary looking. She is a bit
dumpy, she is middle-aged, but she is the one who loves
God. There is a sense that this is the real thing."

We must look closely at these two dreams. In the first,
the pawing, mauling dog with its great teeth threatening
her eyes—her consciousness—is her home-grown image
of instinctual aggression gone unheeded, of potential
destruction that she dare not deny, or it will savage her.
She cannot just knuckle under and be a good little girl or
the dog will control her through her fear of it. She must
wrestle to house the dog, to house this aggressiveness as

if it were a dog she had to tame and train and leash, but always recognizing it as other, as not entirely domesticated or harnessed to conscious purpose. Its bigness, and its particular animal state as a dog link it symbolically to the wild, dark Hecate, goddess of the underworld. Such an archetypal reality can never be completely summed up and put in place by conscious intention. The dream task is to house this energy, to make a space in consciousness for it, not to own it, to possess it or gut it.

If she does not struggle to house it, where will the dog go? Out on the neighbor's lawn, or worse, onto the neighbor's children, or to strike at the neighbor's eyes. The images that are alive in us do not just go away if we neglect them; they go unconscious. In the unconscious they accumulate more and more force, and regress to more and more archaic forms, the more they are denied the intercession of the ego.[11] The ego's ministry is to pay attention to such images, to make space for them in consciousness. That allows such images to be modified by contact with reality. Then we can use this aggressive energy, whether in the world or to sustain a further reach into the unconscious.

Social oppression is always fueled by the psychological repression of what we do not struggle to house. What we repress poisons the psychological and spiritual atmosphere, like acid rain. What we repress pollutes the genuine feelings and thoughts we do express, by intruding into them a hidden motive, hidden even from ourselves, that twists what we say and mean to ulterior purposes. What we repress amasses energy in our unconscious like a private weapons arsenal and explodes into the world whether through a sniper's bullet, a burst of unrestrained anger out of proportion to its cause, or a gust of emotion that inflates a small spark of controver-

sy into uncontrollable size. What we repress will even-
tually join together with what others repress, as together
we seek a scapegoat to unload itself upon. Sooner or later,
if we do not deal with the untamed dog, we will select a
group onto whom the dog will be loosed. In fact, we
might even feel justified at unleashing our dog on this
other group. The evil we neglect to admit and fail to
house will amass its strengths, attack, accuse and seek to
make nothing of the connections we hold to be so important in our lives.

We must also account for the next image, from the same
night's dreams, of God who comes down. Yet when
down, it is not God, but she who loves God. There is a
pleasing ambiguity here. She who loves God is the one
who loves by living in her house, seeing what passes
through it, containing what she can and making space for
what is untenable, uncontainable. Is the one who loves
God an ordinary woman called to house the extraordinary presence of God? Is she God in herself or the lover
of God? These are the images the psyche puts to the
dreamer to wrestle with. That is precisely what Jung
reminded us to do: to take seriously what our particular
wrestling with God requires of us. My own thought about
Jung is that he had no place to put the bad, so he put it in
God and wrestled with it there, saying God possessed a
dark side. In psychoanalytic terms we could hazard the
interpretation that Jung struggled to reach what Melanie
Klein called the depressive position, that sorrowful yet
bracing realization that bad and good are mixed through
all of life—in ourselves, in those we love and esteem, in
those upon whom we are dependent.[12] No moral state exists in such simple purity, only in confusing ambiguity. It
is as if Jung could not see how we could house those opposites of love and hate within us, so he saw God hous-

ing them, struggling with them, and needing our help to
do so.

For some of us, the problem is just the reverse. We cannot house the good, so we put it all into God and make a
fixed, idealized God meanwhile feeling only too
alienated, fragmented, and sinful in ourselves, missing
the great joy of faith. We must struggle to house both the
bad and the good. That is the ministry of the ego. The particular images through which this task is handed to us,
that frame our particular questions, are the same kinds of
images and questions asked in the large of all humanity.
How can there be evil and a good God? What can we do
with the reality of evil?

When we try to admit and house evil in ourselves, it
does not get all neatened and straightened up, explained
away. Rather we are opened to the mystery of evil. We
step in line with Jung, behind Job, with our questions,
with his questions in hand. We step in line behind Job,
who steps in line behind Cain and Abel. Why is life like
this? Why do the innocent suffer? In terms of Cain and
Abel, why is one gift accepted and the other refused?
Even though one son was clearly accepted, he fared no
better than the son who was rejected. He was murdered,
after all, as Jesus was later to be crucified. Cain, the son
whose offering Yahweh rejected, was cursed, thrown into
alienation—a homeless, rootless state. Who is this Yahweh who does not deal fairly with the first two brothers,
a God on whose account both suffer?

The temptation, the Devil's trick, leads us from the
mystery of Yahweh, who does not conform to our rules
of fairness, our conceptions of what God ought to be like
but confounds them. The trick would lead us from the
puzzlement and pain of Yahweh's mysterious rejection
and equally mysterious acceptance. The Devil's trick

tempts us to avoid the stark otherness of the transcendent One who simply does not fit into our understanding of fair play, as he drives us away from our terror before this unknown, this untamed God.[13]

Instead of feeling the wound to heart and soul, we, like Cain, fasten on envy of our brother, as if Abel were the origin of the problem. Then we put our revenge or our solution in the center place, pinning ourselves to a false cross. The real cross in that situation is to suffer the shocking hurt and confounding of our rules of justice, to keep our eye on Yahweh. Who is this that accepts me, but I know not why? Who is this that refuses what I bring, but I know not why? The real cross is to stay wrestling there, in that gap between our images of God and God's self-disclosure. The false cross defrauds us of that vision and lures us to accuse our neighbors, as Cain accused Abel, saying "It is your fault! You must pay!"

Job held on right in that crucible of the immediate experience of Yahweh. He held on past the explanations of his friends who tried to fit him to the rules, saying, clearly he suffered because he broke the rules. Job was pushed past all standards of fairness, past all that was known and imagined about God's justice. He was pushed to join with the suffering of the innocent, like those children slaughtered at Christ's birth when, it is said, Christ lost his own innocence.[14] It is not insignificant that at the end of the tale Job becomes the intercessor for just these friends, because he was grounded in more immediate experience of Yahweh and thus opened to Yahweh's self-revelation.[15]

Job kept his eye on Yahweh simply by taking his image of the Lord seriously. Job stands for all of us in doing that and for the best of our human images of God. For Job believed in the God of ethical monotheism, in whom justice forms the core. By holding to this image of God he went straight into the darkness of the questions that Cain shirked: Why does God reject me? Why does God make me suffer? By holding on to his image of God—which represented the best of our human concerns—Job exposed the bankruptcy of all our human versions, visions, and images of God. As Paul Ricoeur puts it, ". . . Job bears witness to the irreducibility of the evil of scandal to the evil of fault"; it cannot be explained.[16] Coming to the end of the ladder of human images for God, Job sees the gap between them and the transcendent One. Job moves to give up the narcissism of his particular point of view to make a leap to something bigger. Yahweh shows him the way of a transcendent God who is not distant now, but speaks directly to Job, addressing questions to him, taking him seriously enough to show him something of divine reality. Thus is Job given an immediate experience of a present God who surpasses all previous human understanding of God. The answer to Job is a constantly more accessible God who comes right to us, who speaks in his own person, who reaches us in love. This God is not a plan of consciousness, not a new mental health scheme, not a political solution, nothing abstract or generalized, but a person.

Where are we left then? Right there in the gap, between our images of God and God's self-disclosure. Like Job, our images of God are lifelines to our psyches, enabling us to hold on in the midst of confusion, of perplexity, and of suffering, to catch our meaning in a net full of great holes, the great rents in the fabric of our individual and shared being.[17] With these lifelines we do not just plunge through the gap into meaninglessness. But as we hold onto our images, to those experiences that have marked us, we are brought to the edge of the unknown. Then they break off, even break down. They cannot reach across. They cannot cover the abyss of unknowing, where God may come to speak to us, to be with us, even appear to us. We are left then living very near this gap, sometimes even falling into it. The burden of the Christian, and of the clergy in particular, is to struggle right there in the gap, where all our knowledge moves into unknowing. We must not deny that mystery, nor indulge in the fiction that the perfect theory would clear it all up, would make it all calm by closing the gap between us and God. When we do that we are no better than Cain. We have taken our eye off Yahweh to pounce on our neighbor to explain why misfortune afflicts the world.

The ministry of the ego, and the ministry of the church, understood as the ego of Christendom, is to get a house for this struggle, to see the reality of evil, to know beyond doubt that it is different from the reality of the good. We cannot accomplish either, the housing or the moral certainty of the good, unless we do both. We need to claim the good in order to house the evil. Otherwise we will be overtaken by evil—burnt out, burnt up. The Devil's trick is to divert us from this ego task, by frightening us with large abstract evils so that we let go of the little devils that live in us. And so we are seduced to forget our petty evils which are our own specific and concrete ego tasks to meet. We see ourselves not only participating in the great production "Evil and the Universe," but starring in it!

Christians have a lot to answer for here, I believe. We are too easily tricked in this way, hearing and saying in words always addressed to us, "Ah, it's selfish to do that. It's bourgeois. It is individualistic, part of the decadence of the West to think about these little problems, a petty elitism." We should be working to change the world. We should be helping in all the great causes, making a brave new world come about quickly. But, too often, what we do in the service of the great causes is to join Job's friends moralizing about evil, making easy, tidy explanations, saying to all around us, if only you had the right political, social, historic, economic understanding, the right connection to the unconscious, or the right kind of piety, the right side, in a word, then none of this would be happening to you or your country or the world, no big dog would be leaping to savage you. Meanwhile, our own dog with its great jaws is joining the pack; we feel ourselves justified in letting it loose on the enemy, and more than justified, required to do so.

Housing evil means not being fobbed off by the Devil's trick into grabbing for the utopian solution. We are painfully aware of the powers of destruction—the violence leaping up in countries all over the world. The Devil tricks us to collaborate with him by looking to solve everything cleanly, quickly, altogether forgetting the Christian wisdom that reminds us that we are flawed, imperfect, always fallible, not perfectible. The opposite temptation, also the Devil's trick, is then to withdraw and do nothing, often under the guise of seeking "a spiritual life." But an unfleshed spiritual life, removed from the ambiguities, stresses, and surprises of living is an ersatz life. Spirit in the flesh is the Christian secret, wrestling with the realities of power, money, conflict, finite limits and finite possibilities. Solving evil or withdrawing from it leads to dead ends. Neither route houses the evil we can identify and do something about. One denies it, and in denying it becomes it; the other resigns to it and thus also becomes it. The alternative is to grasp and to claim the good, not the utopian good, but the good-enough good, which is tough, small, concrete, real. It means recognizing that order always comes out of disorder. The

order that would put an end to disorder is the most
frightening disorder of all, Because freedom always
means mess.

Just as we cannot house evil if we do not claim the
good, we cannot claim and build up the good if we do not
see the evil that besieges us. Evil displays a different
order of being from the good's. Evil destroys being. Good
builds being. It is psychologically and politically sound
that our response to evil, besides the struggle to house it,
is to build up the good against it. The Devil tries to trick
us into not doing that but instead to become so fascinated
with toe-to-toe combat with evil that everything else dis-
appears. We fight evil best by becoming totally involved
in exploring the reality of the good, which is real being.

III.

How do we do that? How do we claim the good and build
it up? I go back again to the concrete and the small in the
example of a woman's dream to which she gave a name.
She called it her "theological dream." It is very short: "I
am placed at the Goodness Table. Not the Safety Table
where my friend is placed, nor the Badness Table. There
is no food at the Badness Table. And there is no one
there." End of dream. The dreamer says about the woman
placed at the Safety Table that she definitely represents a
part of herself that always seeks approval, always tries to
find a politically expedient solution that won't ruffle or
make waves. She knew how strong her own pull was
toward the safety of gaining others' approval. But the
dreamer also saw this other woman as one who sought
power, if not in a political situation, at least over herself.
The dreamer never liked that power-seeking behavior in

her friend. The dream made her understand such motives
in herself and also see that her friend's self-aggrandizing
may have sprung from her wanting always to be safe. The
dreamer was shocked to find that she herself was placed
at the Goodness Table; she would have put herself at the
Badness Table because she was forever fretting over her
inferiorities, her lapses, her faults. It was a penance and
a discipline for her to be seated at the Goodness Table.
What struck her even more strongly was that nothing—
no thing, no food, no one—sat at the Badness Table. She
felt that was the truth about evil. No thing is there, in
place of some thing. No nourishment is offered there. In
contrast, her task was to sit at the Goodness Table and eat.
That was her penance. Through this dream, perhaps we
can all learn that the Devil's trick is to get us not to sit at
the Goodness Table.

To sit at the Goodness Table would mean not being
afraid to say we have made a right decision, even though
it was not a perfect one. It might mean not denying that
our intention toward another was good, even though self-
serving motives were also involved. It might mean admitting that our intention as a nation is to harbor freedom,
to give bountifully to our neighbors around the world,
even though there are self-serving actions and all sorts of
dubious procedures and politics mixed up in this giving.
If we cannot claim the good as it lives in us, we have no
house in which to tame the beast as it leaps up in us. We
only tear down our own house, join our own detractors,
desert the good, leave it homeless, an orphan. What good
exists in us goes begging, altogether neglected. We fear
this view of claiming the good. We think it leads to inflation, pomp, and self-preening.

In the church, too, we can be too quick to point the ac-
cusing finger and too slow to hold out the good bits that

glow there in our tradition, and give not just solace and comfort for suffering, but the glad joy, the amazement at finding diamond-hard truths there, available to us for the asking. Claiming the good means feeling and acknowledging the joy of the good. It means knowing that a dreamer can spot the trick in his dream and get the right issue, seeing that a person in analysis can feel so cared about. Claiming the good means that people like ourselves do get up week after week and talk about the transcendent God who comes down into our midst; it means that we can dream of a God with all that pleasing ambiguity. Is she God? Is God—can God be—a she? Is it she who loves God or is it God who loves her? It is good that the psyche gives us such images. It is good that we are given such dreadful freedom to keep our eye on a God who confounds all our images of God. It is good that there are clergy who throughout all the liturgical year pray for each member of their congregation, expanding their souls' space in the rush of life, so that when they go into their churches they can smell that these are churches that have been prayed in.

We all know these moments of goodness. They are little, they are big, like the smell of fresh bread, or the soothing wetness of water on the skin. They are in the fact that a woman diagnosed as terminally ill finds suddenly settled in her a life-long besetting fear. This liberation allows her in the midst of the great suffering afflicting her to step gladly into moments of ease and joy. After a dozen years of struggle she can give herself whole-heartedly to her love for her husband. Under the shadow of death she finds unexpectedly a glowing light of life-giving love under the nurturing wing of goodness. And all these small and large miracles happen in the midst of filth, in the midst of malice, bombings, murders, and every sort of petty meanness. Building up the good means not letting go of these bits and not refusing them, even though they do not put an end to murder or meanness or malice, but ourselves taking up our assignment at the Goodness Table, and gladly.

We are reluctant to do that because goodness asks things of us, makes its firm claims in turn. Goodness makes the special claim on us of asserting its claims in and through the self we are given, by being fully present to that self, including its evil, its pettiness, its special failures and fallibilities. We need to be fearfully realistic about evil but that does not mean we are to be endlessly fearful.

Goodness says, "Claim me, in yourself, in others, as I show myself in the world. Do not put up endless fronts in place of my being in you, playing parts instead of being present." We evade this true self the way we evade contemplating the infinite. We are too busy, too tired, too preoccupied with the method of arrival ever to give attention to what awaits us there. Thus in prayer we empty and block at the same time. Claiming the good means just that—taking it, letting ourselves receive it and giving it back.[18]

Goodness demands that we take it, accept it, receive it. That means making room for it, being stripped of whatever gets in its way.[19] This is the familiar stage of purgation that we all know about. We must clean house and discover the second, third, fifth, eighth things we have put in the place of the first thing. We must confess that we have turned away, acting as if this bit of goodness had not come to us. We must face the fact that we have perjured the truth that has shown itself to us, living as if it were false. Goodness radiates all the force of created being—burning, actualizing, illuminating, We need to confess the evil we do and that is done to us—all those pulls away from illumination into opaqueness, into fogging over, whirling away into mist far from the center, not caring for it, not daring it.

Confessing our failure to house the good and build it up makes us feel how thoroughly bad is mixed up in all our good motives and makes us in the best sense penitent. It makes us see how even in the evil that is done to us we veer off course away from the good, sinking into our suffering at the hands of others, overcome with bitterness, resentment, and misery. Yet we can still feel rising in us the impulse to make amends, to repair the hurt, to come again to a willing attentiveness and joyful excitement. That in itself is a bit of good in the midst of pain and suffering.

Claiming the good means recognizing its pull, its impulse in us to take it in hand and give what belongs to it back to it by our desire to make things better. We know about these gestures and we are glad to know what we know, the bad and the *good*.

Examples of our impulse to repair are wonderful and plentiful. One I am very fond of comes from a woman I was working with in analysis who had a fine sense of humor. She had turned away from the true self she was given to be and tried to crowbar herself, like Cinderella's sisters, into the wrong shoe, always ending up maiming herself. She was very depressed to realize this. She suffered a great deal. She knew she was perjuring her true self; she knew she was constantly tempted still to do so. She did not know who she really was yet, either. She was tempted into an orgy of bad feeling, about herself, about life, about everything. One of the particularly feminine ways she made amends, gave much of herself back to herself and repaired her broken faith in goodness was to go to Bloomingdale's cosmetics counter and make up her face in new and different ways, not to cover up her depression but to search through it for her true face. Was this face her true face or was that other her proper one? It was her way of playing around and giving back into the whole problem of human identity a circus of rich possibilities for selfhood.

There are other, bigger examples. I think of those rock stars who gave a great free concert to raise money for famine victims in Ethiopia, and perhaps doing penance for all that noisy music they have let loose into our streets and in the violence of feeling both of those that like it and those that hate it. I think of a former student working as a chaplain in a city hospital, specifically for AIDS patients, whom everybody else treats like lepers. I remember a sister and brother who, in their early teens, lost their beloved mother. She was the only person through whom they felt any of the goodness of life. The daughter was so overcome by their loss and suffering that she took her treasured photographs of her mother and gave them to her brother. Feeling her grief so keenly, she gave it over into solace for his grief. There really are countless examples of goodness. All of us know them. They happen over and over again, and in them we can feel God coming down into our midst, if only for an instant. Then each of us, male and female, is she who loves God.

Claiming the good means bearing gladly the joy of these moments, the flickers of joy that do not often enough go out visibly into this dark, anxious world we live in. This unmitigated darkness is the world God enters, lives in, and saves. In it we are assigned seats at the Goodness Table. If we refuse what is offered, the good that is given us, the seats at the table, we do not live the

will of God but fall for the Devil's tricks. If we do take
our seat there, choosing it over and over again, we live a
life that is a song of praise.

NOTES

1. Corresponding with grace is a mysterious part of
   religious life and an essential one. Grace in this sense
   is the gift that enables one to take what God offers, to
   receive it willingly, to lay hold of it aggressively. We
   write: "Corresponding to the good—to grace—means
   cooperating with the parts given us, using them and
   seeing ourselves as being used, trying to fit them this
   way and that into the whole puzzle." We go on to say
   "Accepting the good bit given is the way we correspond to the good, which comes to us as grace,
   something that happens which we could not bring
   about by our efforts alone, but which intimately connects with the efforts we do make, confirming them,
   making them succeed. Grace does not cancel or substitute for our own efforts because it does not depend
   on them. The paradox of grace consists in both its
   making actual what we strove for but could not
   achieve and its coming as something very different
   from what we thought we wanted. Grace surprises us
   as always more than we expected and as coming from
   the most unlikely corners of our lives. While it comes
   entirely in its own terms, it endorses us, recognizing
   what we tried to do." Ann and Barry Ulanov, *Cinderella and Her Sisters: The Envied and the Envying* (Philadelphia: Westminster Press, 1983), pp. 147, 148–149.
2. The term "dream-ego" refers to our representation of
   self in our dreams, when we dream of ourselves as an

"I." Often on waking, we naively assume an exact equation or identity between our waking and our dreaming egos, between the *I* of everyday life and the very different dream "I." But dreams show us something quite different. The psyche in dreams shows us pictures of our ego that correct our conscious stance or reveal its hidden inflation, for example, or show us another way we might react to a situation that traps us into making stereotyped responses in our waking life. Although a close relation exists between our waking and dreaming egos, they simply are not identical and much can be learned from looking closely into the gap between them. We can see, for example, how our ego-stance looks to the psyche, from the psyche's own point of view. Jung's method of subjective interpretation—of inquiring what a dream figure represents in the dreamer's own psyche, even though that figure exists as an actual person in the dreamer's waking life—needs to be applied to the dream-ego too.

To take a familiar example, when we dream we are trying to control a car we are driving but it mysteriously goes backwards out of control, all our efforts to clamp down on the brakes notwithstanding, the dream shows us trying to be in control and panicking when we are not. It shows us our fear we will go backwards if we remain out of control, back toward what we cannot see, back into the past, back into that unconscious world where conscious sight does not look. It hints of a secret connection between control and loss of control, between pressing forward and regression, between our conscious doing and our unconscious undoing. The waking ego by recalling the dream-ego's plight may gain us elbow room, a margin of freedom, from the complex of panic over loss of control or even the threat of it. The picture of the dream-ego allows us to inquire as to which archetypal image informs it. Do we as drivers embody an heroic ego? Or are we victims striving against victimhood and failing? What purpose does the psyche aim for in presenting this image to us of our dreaming self? Does the dream-ego gain through its failure to drive the car as it releases us from the plans and plots of consciousness? Is the dream-ego trying to re- connect us to the unconscious psyche? Can it only do that under the guise of losing control, in regression, in its inability to take over and drive the car because of tyrannical control by the waking-ego?

The task in this sort of interpretation is to give both the dream-ego and the waking-ego their due. James Hillman explores the life of the dream-ego liberated from the conscious ego in an interesting way, though I think he tips too far toward the unconscious. With luck we expand to house both the waking-ego, as it lives in the world in shared experience with others, and the dream-ego as it moves among the inner population of which it is a part, within the unconscious. See James Hillman, *The Dream and the Underworld* (San Francisco: Harper & Row, 1979), pp. 94–96.

3. For additional examples of persons' images of the Devil, see Ann Belford Ulanov, "The Psychological Reality of the Demonic" and "Heaven and Hell" in *Picturing God*, pp. 134–135, 156.

4. For a discussion of such experiences, see Ann and Barry Ulanov, *Religion and the Unconscious*, pp. 13 ff. St. Augustine offers many examples of such gripping moments in his own life. See Barry Ulanov, *The Pray-*

ers of St. Augustine (San Francisco: Harper & Row, 1983).

5. Klein writes, "Love is not absent in the criminal, but it is hidden and buried in such a way that nothing but analysis can bring it to light; since the hated persecuting object was originally to the tiny baby the object of all its love and libido, the criminal is now in the position of hating and persecuting his own loved object; as this is an intolerable position all memory and consciousness of any love for any object must be suppressed. If there is nothing in the world but enemies, and that is how the criminal feels, his hate and destructiveness are, in his view, to a great extent justified—an attitude which relieves some of his unconscious feelings of guilt. Hate is often used as the most effective cover for love. . . ." Melanie Klein, "On Criminality," in *Love, Guilt, and Reparation and Other Works 1921–1945* (New York: Delacorte/Seymour Lawrence Press, 1975), p. 260.

6. Kierkegaard describes the suffering of "shut-upness": "The demoniacal is *shut-upness . . . unfreely revealed.* These two traits denote, as they should, the same thing; for the shut-up is precisely the mute, and if it has to express itself, this must come about against its will when the freedom lying prone in unfreedom revolts upon coming into communication with freedom outside and now betrays unfreedom in such a way that it is the individual who betrays himself against his will in dread. . . . Freedom is precisely the expansive. It is in opposition to this I would employ the word "shut-up," *kat' exochen,* for "unfreedom." Commonly, a more metaphysical term is used for the evil. It is called "negating." The ethical term precisely corre-

sponding to that, when one contemplates the effect thereof upon the individual, is shut-upness. The de-moniacal does not shut itself up *with* something, but shuts *itself* up, and in this lies the mystery of existence, the fact that unfreedom makes a prisoner precisely of itself. . . . When freedom then comes in contact with shut-upness it becomes afraid. . . .

". . . The only power which can compel shut-upness to speak is either a higher demon . . . or the good which is absolutely able to be silent." Søren Kierkegaard, *The Concept of Dread*, trans. Walter Lowrie (Princeton: Princeton University Press, 1957), pp. 110–111.

See also Ann Belford Ulanov, "The Psychological Reality of the Demonic," in *Picturing God*, pp. 139–140, for further discussion of the state of "shut-upness."

A further word can be said about the confounding confusion of the true and the false cross. Even the most established healing procedures, such as psycho-analysis, can collude with a false vision, or worse, per-petuate a false vision of its deepest aim of facilitating a person's capacity for real living. Masud Khan sums this up: "In our clinical work, sometimes, it is more important to sustain a person in living than to rid him of his illness. Winnicott . . . summed this up in his statement, '. . . absence of psycho-neurotic illness may be health, but it is not life'. . . .

"The demand for *life*, and if that is not possible, for not *living*, is made upon us by the patient and is not a bias of our restitutive omnipotence as therapists. When a patient makes this demand upon us, we have every right to *refuse* it, but not to confuse it. The patient is willing to stay ill and suffer the consequences so long as he or she is *living* or *not living*. If we try to sub-vert his life by a cure, he either escapes us or gives up

his right to be alive and ill and enters into a complicity
with us that we mistake for 'treatment alliance.' Gilles
Deleuze . . . in spite of his mocking acerbity, raises an
important issue. He argues that Melanie Klein establishes a contract with her patients in which the
patients bring their intense experiences of living and
she translates them into fantasies for them. . . . With
Winnicott the point is reached when one has to share
with the patient his experience. Deleuze asks whether
this is a question of sympathy, empathy, or identification. He concludes: 'What we feel is rather the necessity of a relationship which is neither legal,
contractual or institutional.'" M. Masud R. Khan,
"Secret as Potential Space," in *Hidden Selves*, p. 97.

7. The Freudian analyst Hans Loewald's understanding
    of transference bears on this phenomenon of the real
    cross. To say we transfer past experiences and uncon-
    scious experiences into present relationships is not to
    say the past and the unconscious exist as set contents
    in some separate region of the psyche. Instead, says
    Loewald, "In its fundamental meaning, unconscious
    is the name for a mode of experiencing or mentation
    that continually, throughout life, constitutes the active
    base and source of more differentiated and more com-
    plexly organized modes of mentation." In fact, he con-
    tinues, the past is not really ours unless we are
    constantly reworking and recombining it with our
    present experiences: "What I call my unconscious
    memories and impulses are potentially mine to the ex-
    tent to which they may be raised to a new level of men-
    tation, may become integrated with the context of my
    conscient mode of experiencing." But this process of
    "appropriation" and "translation" works both ways:
    ". . . there is a need for conscient appropriation of un-

conscious experience as well as a need for reappropri-
ating conscient modes (and the corresponding mental
contents) into unconscious mental activity—and back
again toward consciousness." Transference, then, occurs not just between people, but also between the id
and ego, and it plays an essential role in our humanness: "What counts is this live communication, a
mutual shaping, a reciprocal conforming of levels of
mentation. The richer a person's mental life is, the
more translation occurs back and forth between unconscious and conscious experience. To make the
unconscious conscious, is one-sided. It is the transference between them that makes a human life, that
makes life human."

Transference between people, and especially of
erotic feelings, brings into play the historical and ongoing activity of each person in becoming a self in
himself or herself. Each person is working over, ap-
propriating and translating experiences back and
forth between consciousness and unconsciousness, a
process that we all know involves suffering as well as
growing. This "work" amounts to owning all of our
experience, accepting its wounding and thus also enduring its cross-like impact. Loewald writes, "Love,
then, is a force or power that not only brings people
together, one person loving another, but equally
brings oneself together into that one individuality
which we become through our identifications."

The richness of life, even its very meaning, according to Loewald, is to be found in this multi-layered interpenetration of types of conscious and unconscious
mentation within us and between us: "Consciousness
of transference means that the living interpenetration
of lives past and present can be resumed. . . . It is this

interplay between unconscious and consciousness, between past and present, between the intense density of undifferentiated, inarticulate experience and the lucidity of conscious articulate experience, that gives meaning to our life. Without such meaning-giving play we have no future of our own. Perhaps what we call man's symbolizing activity is that play."

Thus to own all levels of our experiencing and bring them into play with other persons, and receiving their full experiencing too, is willingly to enter into the goodness and the suffering of existence. It means to refuse the temptation of over-simplification and to accept the weight of our complex historicity, especially when conflicts arise in our lives. The real cross is indeed real. Accepting it means to go on experiencing the interpenetration of many aspects of living (and dying) in ourselves and others. It means to go on working on these complex interrelationships and to be surprised and glad when bits of grace interrupt and confirm this work, See Hans Loewald, "Transference and Love," in *Psychoanalysis and the History of the Individual* (New Haven: Yale University Press, 1978), pp. 30, 31, 40, 49–50.

8. I am indebted for this example to Professor Emeritus J. Louis Martyn of Union Theological Seminary, New York City.

9. See, for example, C. G. Jung, *Psychology and Religion in Psychology and Religion: West and East, Collected Works,* Vol. 11, trans. R.F.C. Hull (New York: Pantheon, 1958), p. 168, par. 247; see also C. G. Jung, "Foreword to White's *God and the Unconscious,*" in *Psychology and Religion: West and East,* pp. 304 ff., par. 456–9; see also C. G. Jung, "Foreword to Werblowsky's *Lucifer and Prometheus,*" in *Psychology and Religion: West and East,*

pp. 313 ff., par. 470. Jung writes of the two sides of his own experience of God, the good and the bad: "The attribute 'coarse' is mild in comparison to what you feel when God dislocates your hip or when he slays your first born. . . .

That is *one* side of my experiences with what is called 'God.' 'Coarse' is too weak a word for it. 'Crude,' 'violent,' 'cruel,' 'bloody,' 'hellish,' 'demonic' would be better. That I was not downright blasphemous I owe to my domestication and polite cowardice. And at each step I felt hindered by a beatific vision of which I'd better say nothing." C. G. Jung *Letters*, ed. Gerhard Adler and Aniela Jaffé, trans. R. F. C. Hull (Princeton: Princeton University Press, 1975), Vol. 2, p. 156.

10. Karl Barth, *Church Dogmatics: The Doctrine of Reconciliation*, trans. and ed. by G. W. Bromiley and T. F. Torrance (Edinburgh: T. & T. Clark, 1961), Vol. IV, 3, #69, p. 178. See also Karl Barth, *Church Dogmatics: The Doctrine of Creation*, Vol. III, 3, #50, pp. 289–368. See also Robert P. Scharlemann, "The No to Nothing and the Nothing to Know: Barth and Tillich and the Possibility of Theological Science," *Journal of the American Academy of Religion*, Vol. LV, No. 1, Spring 1987, pp. 57–72. I am indebted to Christopher Morse, Associate Professor of Systematic Theology, Union Theological Seminary, New York City, for this reference.

Envy is a good example of the power of evil to make something into nothing. When we envy we want to spoil or even destroy the good that another shows forth. A person afflicted with envy says, in effect, if I own no goodness no one can, and, if I possess goodness no one else can! For further discussion, see Ann and Barry Ulanov, *Cinderella and Her Sisters: The Envied and the Envying*, chapter 2.

11. For discussion of the ego's intercessory role, see Ann and Barry Ulanov, *Religion and the Unconscious*, chapter 11.

12. For this notion of the dark side of God, see C. G. Jung, *Answer to Job*, in *Psychology and Religion: West and East*, pp. 365, 381, 433, 455, 461, pars. 561, 595n, 694, 739, 747. For description of the depressive position, see Melanie Klein, "The Emotional Life of the Infant," in *Envy and Gratitude and Other Works 1946–1963* (Delacorte Press/Seymour Lawrence, 1975), pp. 71–80.

13. R. C. Zaehner calls it "Our Savage God" in the book by that name (New York: Sheed and Ward, 1974).

14. See Ann Belford Ulanov, "Disguises of the Good," in *Picturing God*.

15. For discussion of this point, see Barry Ulanov, "Job and His Comforters," in *The Bridge, A Yearbook of Judaeo-Christian Studies*, Vol. III, ed. John M. Oesterreicher (New York: Pantheon, 1958).

16. Paul Ricoeur, *The Symbolism of Evil*, trans. Emerson Buchanan (New York: Harper & Row, 1967), p. 314.

17. See Ann Belford Ulanov, "Anxiety of Being," in *The Thought of Paul Tillich*, eds. James Luther Adams, Wilhelm Pauck, Roger Lincoln Shinn (San Francisco: Harper & Row, 1985). There I discuss Tillich's analysis of the anxiety of non-being (as fate, meaninglessness, condemnation) from an opposite point of view, as anxiety to receive the being that is given us to be.

18. See Ann and Barry Ulanov, *Cinderella and Her Sisters: The Envied and the Envying*, chapters 12, 13, 14.

19. Purgation is recognized by many adepts in spiritual transformation as a necessary beginning step in spir-

itual development. Purgation, illumination, union are not merely conventional terms to mark developmental changes; they sum up the great sweep of change that takes place in a fullness of spiritual experience.

WOMEN'S WILES

I.

What the world calls women's wiles have been thought
to be negative—by the world and even more particularly
by religion. Woman is blamed for all the trouble. Eve
looked, Eve listened. She took the fruit from the serpent;
she gave it to Adam. She could be beguiled. And she
beguiled man, who, though maybe a bit slow with less initiative and imagination, was definitely on the straight
and narrow. Woman in contrast was wily, beguiling and
beguilable. Etiologically, wiles and wiliness are linked to
witchcraft, the province of that alien female figure on the
borders of the human community who strikes dread in
both women and men, and also astonishes by creating altogether new mixtures of the known and the unknown.[1]
   Eve is the one who is open, curious, imaginative, wanting. She is the part of the primordial human in all of us
that is desiring, interested, receiving, and thus temptable.
The feminine she symbolizes has been held contemptible
as a result. She is the feminine we fear because it can be
so easily beguiled. Yet, Eve was in fact after wisdom, prudent practical wisdom, wasn't she? Mary took into her
heart this God who had taken up residence in her. She
housed what she saw and heard and she became the
house, the church, for us all. In a womanly way she held
the spirit in her heart, not fleeing, not solving, not denying, not simply affirming, but pondering it, looking upon

it, making space for it. She knows in her womanliness,
her hiddenness, what can be touched, reached and held
onto, past all the ways we would make that god into our
own image.

Is that the same wisdom that turns up again in Mat-
thew 10, when Jesus is counseling his disciples as they go
out into a world of wolves: "Be wise as serpents"? Don't
we need the wisdom Eve was after to face the Devil's
tricks? Isn't that the same imagination and initiative that
is found in Mary, who takes the revelation and incarnation announced to her, all the way down inside herself
and remains loyal to it, even though she must break con-
ventions and face being made homeless as she gives her
scandalous birth on the borders of human community,
and must flee to a foreign country to keep her child from
being murdered, with a child who, after all this, she does
not really understand? Why does he leave her and Joseph
and stay in the temple, this child who as a man she sees
naked, hanging on the cross, stripped of all powers, all
projections, all hope?

We need what Mary and Eve symbolize of the feminine
modality of being. We need that wiliness, that prudent
practical wisdom, the images the psyche hands us, in
order to do the work of housing, to be able to keep up the
struggle, to keep our eye on Yahweh, who breaks all our
images. We need that beguiling and steadfast toughness
to evade the Devil's tricks and to build up the good. We
need what Eve and Mary symbolize of the way that goes
down into the midst of what is, into the ground of the
beliefs that inhabit us, into fear, terror, and that defeating
sense of not belonging. We know, living in this mode, that
we are Eve, dazzleable, temptable, tricked into taking
something that turns out to be a nothingness that somehow fills the world, forsaking what we thought was noth-

ing that turns out to be everything precious, now suddenly lost to us. The feminine mode goes right down into the
moral ambiguity of life, into the matriarchal superego, in
contrast to the patriarchal. Instead of going up into
abstractions and pluperfectly clear discriminations
(which have their place, are also useful, and not to be
thrown out), the matriarchal superego originates right
there in our earliest and most immediate experiences,
before consciousness has firmly established itself. Thus it
is strongly marked by the tonalities of the unconscious.
It shows the savagery of intense instinctual drives, needs,
desires, and ambitions. It shows a voracious appetite to
touch and incorporate, to get all mixed up in others, just
as our loving and hating mix inside us. The feminine
mode of being is not all cozy and cheery. It is a fierce force,
a primordial one. The judgments we make from the
matriarchal superego are not simple, fixed, universalized
like those of the patriarchal superego, but rather possess
the "both- and," ambivalent quality of reality "in the in-
determinate tonalities of lived experience where love and
hate go together. . . ."[2] The matriarchal superego takes us
down into those places where we wrestle with our images, where we live in the gap, between images and
reality, where we try to put bad and good together, not always succeeding, but always trying, going on somehow.

This feminine way had, for centuries and for countless
people, been projected upon the figure of Mary and carried and contained there. In our century, many, especially in the Protestant churches, have withdrawn this
projection. We must ask: Where has all this energy gone?
Where is it turning up? For as I said, the feminine mode
is not all cozy and comfortable. It is a brute primordial
force. Mary is not just meek and mild, but vigorous,
daring, aggressive, the mother of the great revolution, for

it is she who bears into the world the One who ends all
religions. Perhaps we have lost Mary as a container for
this energy because she was separated from her own
darkness, her own woman's wiles, from the country of
the witch. The witch herself became distorted by being
made all negative, separated from her embodiment of a
feminine power and intellect that brought original insight into the world.[3] Mary became all light and the witch
became all dark. That is not good. We need her wily side.

A contemporary man's dream makes this point about
the necessity of the witch to the feminine in all of us. He
was facing a very serious oral examination in his professional life. There were a number of people examining him
on anything they pleased. He was terrified by the ordeal.
He was doubly terrified by the fear that he would be
tempted to play a good little boy to try to please his examiners. He knew enough from previous experience of
these teachers that that would be fatal. They would have
him by the throat. In preparing himself psychologically
for this exam, he had the following dream:

He said: "I go to buy books. The man selling them says
that it is possible to get an original edition and returns
with the one I want most in the original text. It is a marvelous deep brown tome with scroll or parchment pages
with the script magically pressed into them. As I look at
it I see this script is alive, and written by X (a woman in
his life he thinks of as possessed of wisdom and
authority). It is volume four of forty-four volumes so
there is a lot more to go on reading." As he reads, the text
becomes a living scene. He explains the scene: "I see X in
her younger life when she is still forming herself. The text
I am reading refers to witches and in particular about a
witch in X's own being that she must come to terms with.
The text is now like real life and I see X younger, vul-

nerable, even hysterical and distraught, struggling with the witch in her own life. She is so different there from the X I know, who seems so calm and wise." End of dream. He woke up feeling, if X can do it, so can I. He saw X dealing with this threat of the witch on the witch's "most awful level," and then writing about it in the living script of the dream. X's calm, wise authority springs from facing the witch and assimilating the encounter gradually into readable form, not as dead information but as living experience. He saw he needed both resources to draw upon when he was being tested—the calm, wise feminine and the cunning, aggressive witch who knew how to fight. So he took into the exam with him his wits and his wiles, ready to sting his examiners with a magic finger, if necessary, like a witch turning them into toads, ready to speak with authority of what he knew and of what he had done with what he knew, that is, out of his original mixtures of the known and unknown.

As for us, where has all this feminine energy gone that used to be projected upon and contained in Mary? It is interesting to speculate about it. It has gone into the depths, I think, creating the new discipline of depth psychology. Women have had everything to do with this new discipline. They have been its material prima. In a far larger proportion than men, women have risked going down into lived experience, both conscious and unconscious, and exposed their hidden depths to inspection. Women have not only been patients, but many of the early and present practitioners in this discipline have been female, going at their work in distinctly female ways.[4] An equally important fact about depth psychology is the enormous amount of energy devoted in it to feminine modes of being. For a number of decades depth psychology has focused in the most direct way on the pivotal impact of

the mother in forming being in her children. We must
recognize with gratitude the work of Jung, Melanie Klein,
and D. W. Winnicott, all of whom, for a great many good
reasons, have differentiated the maternal from actual
women. Mothers no longer loom as villains here, making
possible or impossible their children's lives, causing
neurosis and psychosis in their offspring. In each of these
theorists, however different their ways, there is a frank
and forceful recognition that the child comes into the
world with its own fantasies of good and bad, its own archetypal images of the positive and negative mother, and
the clearest understanding that the child, in its own
temperament and constitution, makes up half of what
Winnicott calls the mother-child couple. We can, all of us,
understand now that it is in relationship to what the child
brings, as well as to what the mother brings, that the
kinds and styles of mothering are made possible or impossible.[5]

This feminine mode of being goes ever more deeply
into the depths. In the recent decades, depth psychology
has moved past its emphasis on the mother to an even
earlier point of investigating the origins of being itself.
How can one be at all? How can there be a self? How does
a self come into being? These questions—psychological,
philosophical, religious—recall all the ancient puzzles:
What is the origin of our being? How can being be sustained? What is the meaning and power of being? Heinz
Kohut investigates the assault on any hold on being by a
disordered narcissism. Otto Kernberg traces the grave
difficulties of our ever arriving at a coherent sense of the
being in persons suffering from the borderline condition.[6] To establish and maintain any sense of being calls
on those feminine modes of being—being at the core of
oneself, being as being-one-with-another, being as pos-

sessed of a personal continuity, knowing that one goes on being.[7]

These modes that are ways of nurturing being have been taken up in thought and conjecture by many in relation to the earth itself, the *mater* of all life. How can we *be* with the earth, sustain its being, not rape it of its resources? How can we be-one-with animal and plant life so that they can go on being? This sensitivity to the feminine mode of holding in being has gained intensity with respect to the whole global human family. How can we protect being-at-the-core in all people, recognizing that we are fundamentally the same human creatures? How can this search for shared origins reach through conflicts of racial, national, and religious differences so that we can be one-with-each-other?

But the feminine mode of being, we must remember, is full of wiles, witchcraft, savage energies. We have in our century gone down into those energies and found out how to explode them into incendiary light, letting loose nuclear energy with all its threats and possibilities. We have seen too in our century the letting loose publicly of forces of sexuality and aggression formerly held behind superego manners and prohibitions. We too easily forget that these forces are also part of the feminine mystery. That is why they are associated with the symbolism of the goddesses. On the streets of New York City where I live, you can feel a tremendous untamed spirit that is abroad—restless, dynamic, but unhoused and hence wildly volatile, altogether unpredictable. It could break out at any moment and all too often does in acts of savage violence—murders, muggings, senseless maimings, rape. Sexual signs show up on almost every street corner advertising quick availability in inverse proportion to a decrease in its sharing of intimacy. We need all the wiles of Eve and Mary to survive in a world outside the borders of Eden. All this energy let loose in our century and not yet adequately housed bears in upon us the truth that life is tragic, a mixture of good and bad. We do terrible things to each other, and terrible things happen to us, things we cannot fix or make right, things which make up a history which cannot just be wiped clean.

We see this feminine energy in our religion too, religion that insistently seeks connection, not abstraction, recognition of the particular, not willing to subsume it always into the universal. Almost all the theologies of recent decades clamor to know—Is God in our midst? Is God coming down the stairs? Does God know my experience of color? My experience of sexual inclination? My experience of being old? Of being young? Of this culture or that political system?

The feminine symbolizes that route that seeks the center by being firmly in the midst of things, touching, immersing oneself.[8] When this mode of approach is lost, repressed, or split off, we lose our ability to feel connected, to feel in a living way that what we inherit from the storehouse of our religious tradition matters, that we really can live from the source. For many the distance from religious tradition is so great that they doubt its truth. Religion then goes up into our heads, and we live at a great distance from what matters, caught up instead in psychological formulations, political slogans, religious moralizings. We indulge in and we inflict a guilt upon each other that does not bring remorse and reparation, but only hardens our hearts like the Pharoah's until we close up inside into a fist against ourselves, our neighbor, and God. We withdraw a great distance from everything and everybody, to think everything out, looking at everyone through a sort of scanning ray of consciousness. But we lose as a result the dark mirror, as St. Paul called it, through which we behold our mystery.

We can also withdraw from the center by plunging into movements, into causes, fabricating politicized emotions for ourselves. We do not relate to the images the psyche might toss up to us, but become them instead in a grim identification. Our distance is hidden by our identification. If we become our images in place of holding to our center, we veer off into fanaticism and theological bullying. Yet if we take only the traditional images and neglect to link them to the psychic images that inhabit us, then at best we get a religion of form not of substance, of correct observance pasted over and nullifying our passionate idiosyncratic beliefs. We, individually and in our congregations, fall through the gap in these times of crises.

The down-going feminine way we neglect revenges itself by dragging us down into the dark abyss of matter because we neglect what matters. Symbols regress into symbolic equations and we are easily overtaken by a massing of energy in the unconscious that can at any time explode into neurosis, or into the demand for actual weapons with which we can kill others, or even the whole planet.[9] When we neglect the feminine way that seeks connection we are dragged down into tedious, and interminable procedures, pseudo-connections—endless meetings, memos, position papers, agendas, and votings where nothing significant ever gets said. This particular revenge burgeons in the academic and the business worlds, in government, in the church. The clergy's most particular ministry means going right into that gap between our personal god-images, our group god-images on the one hand, and traditional images from the

storehouse of our tradition on the other.[10] The clergy
needs its feminine wiles and feminine mode of ministry,
not just females taking on a male ministry.

Jung is helpful here, reminding us with his researches
that the ego's job is to relate to the center called the self.
Experience of the self is the marvelous sense of coming
in upon your own subjectivity as an objectively existing
subject, one that addresses you, confronting, confounding, and consoling. Connection to the self is the source of
god-images within us. They arise from the darkness of
the unconscious and from the flesh of ordinary life—our
history of relationships and our culture. These images
reflect our yearning for God, that hope for a life which is
unmistakably alive and real which we bring to the
Eucharist and offer up in our prayers. We need feminine
wiles and the feminine mode of being to house these images and to perform the ego's ministry to connect them
with God's self-revelation.

II.

Women are the ones pressing the question about the missing feminine (and the missing masculine, because if we
lose access to one we skew relation to the other). Including the feminine is something at once subtle and decisive.
It is wily, not straightforward, beguiling, not blunt. But it
is absolutely decisive, like leaven in the lump, that once
included changes the whole. An example illustrates this.
A clergy woman on the standing committee of her
denomination was reviewing with her colleagues, most
of them men, candidates coming up for ordination. At
this meeting she found herself filling up with rage at her

male colleagues because of the questions they were putting to one of the female candidates. The candidate was pregnant, quite pregnant, in fact. The candidate's husband had just gotten a new job and she herself was about to take a new church. The committee men asked with sincere kindness and concern how she was going to put all these parts of her life together. How would she manage with a baby coming, a new church, a new job? At that point the clergy woman got really mad. It took her a while to figure out why. "That is the wrong question," she said. "The parts already go together. Asking that question, however sincerely, makes the parts fall apart. It makes doubt come in. The better question to ask is, How do the parts already fit together? What are the patterns of interaction between them?"

The clergy woman saw the matrix, the embeddedness, the connecting tissue of the candidate's life. Only from that point of view, she recognized, could the questions about parts be asked and the problems be considered. To separate the parts and thus imply they are extractable bits that can be considered abstractly and then to question whether they can ever be put together was destructive. They already existed together as expressions of the woman's life in the world. For all their kind concern, the committee men were demoralizing the candidate, failing to recognize her integrity, not seeing that all the parts arose out of her and came together in her as a whole. They were together. They did not need to be put together. This is a subtle but decisive difference. With this recognition one can see that conflicts of career and family, of clergy meetings and children's bedtimes, for example, point to new solutions, new modes of being, an enlarged life that is more than just a dealing with difficult problems posed by conflicting parts.

The challenge of feminists to the Judeo-Christian tradition offers another example of looking for the missing
feminine element. They ask bluntly: How can our religion
speak to women when God is pictured as male and the
language and iconography are masculine? Where is the
feminine in the credal recital of the Trinity, of God the
Father, Christ the Son, and the Holy Spirit referred to as
He or It? Some women have responded (as others have
responded at other times of conflict in church history) by
forming a separatist movement. They have left the
church. Others have tried to work within the tradition to
uncover the neglected or repressed feminine that lies
latent there. Others have worked to change the major images and language of religious experience and theological discourse.[11]

I want to look at these issues in the same terms I have
been using all through these lectures, in terms of the gap
between our human images for God and the images given
us by tradition. Again, I start with a particular example,
a woman of the clergy, for whom all the parts did go
together. She was married, a parent, and was good at her
job as pastor of her own church. All the parts clearly went
together—except the central one. She felt an emptiness at
the core. Something vital was missing, some lively connection to the center. There a big hole engulfed her. She
tried to fill it by compulsive eating binges. The binges
only resulted in her being drawn further into her emptiness instead of finding connection at the center. She felt
dead. All her duties, all her parts, began to weigh heavily upon her. She could not find the fire in herself, though
others found the way to the fire through her. One place it
beckoned to her strongly was sexually. There she could
feel a spark, a sense of play ignited, a challenge to join the
dance between the sexes. She felt quickened, connected

in the flesh to the spirit, gladly grateful to God. But she could not house this fire in her daily life, which more and more bogged down under her sense of duty. And so she was tempted beyond the circle of her life into liaisons where she did not have to be anyone's mother or wife or pastor, spiritual director, committee member, or meal provider, laundress, financial partner, or community leader. In these flirtations she felt free—only, and completely, herself.

Struggling with these attractions, a dream came to her where she saw herself in another profession. She saw herself as a journalist, free to travel, to make any kind of contact with people. On her way to some assignment, she passes a strange man and between them that ignition strikes that spark, that electricity. They go off to have some sort of sexual meeting. But as they begin, the dream-man takes an iron figure of a cross set within a circle, and attacks her with it, trying to brand her face with the cross. She kicks at him and fights him off and escapes. In the last scene of the dream, she is back at her church, working with another woman, planning new and imaginative ways to gain new members, to bring new members into the congregation.

We can see from the dream that sexuality had slipped through the gap. That was the missing piece. She needed all her wiles not to be seduced into outright condemnation of her own sexual impulses, despite the fact the dream painted them as attracting her to an outsider, the unknown dream-man, the violent intruder. She needed all her wiles not to pull on that particular strand in the Judeo-Christian tradition that stands ready to condemn her sexuality as a dangerous disfigurement of being. She needed to see all that the dream was showing her—that this electricity, this fiery connection, can arise anywhere, anytime. What was clear was that it needed to be housed. Perhaps, it was to be one of the new members to be brought in to the church.[12]

Another central element of our being that also falls through the gap, particularly often with women, is aggression. In one notable dream, a woman dreamt that she was sick and had to go to the hospital for tests. Something was the matter with her heart, the doctor said. His diagnosis was that she had a condition known as Amazon Heart. "It means," she said, "it's enlarged. It means I'm neither female nor male, but more female than male. I go to find Y, a man with whom I'm clearly a woman." End of dream. To Amazon, she associated the warrior woman, the aggressive huntress, a male kind of female. The dream sets her the task of housing this big heart in herself generally and in particular in her womanliness. If she acknowledges this warrior-like hunting aggression, will she still know that she is a woman? When she goes to see Y, the man who makes her feel her own femaleness, does she project her male-like warrior aggression onto him and keep the female part for herself? Doesn't the dream set her the task of housing both the female and male elements in herself? Doesn't the dream go even further and say that her warrior-like aggression is female, in an Amazon figure, not male?

These are particular examples, but not untypical in my experience, nor unimportant, because they clearly illustrate the large issues facing women. These are the sorts of experiences that make many women blame and accuse religious tradition for excluding them, that make many women turn toward the image of the goddess. For there, sexuality and aggression fit into the symbolism of polytheist worship and the female figures prominently in the pantheon of deities.

The goddess images and the assertions they contain are not to be dismissed hastily, nor with scorn, but understood. From a psychological point of view, goddess images recover to all of our consciousness the real value of women's experience and the symbolic value of the feminine in men as well as women. Goddess images touch again the natural forces of life, which too often our Christian heritage seems to brand as outlawed or as an amazon heart that will make us sick. These images join the line of wily wisdom stretching through Mary and Eve back to the serpent. In terms of psychological development, goddess images reach back before the oedipal god-image, to the pre-oedipal god of ambivalent love and hate, of good and bad, fierceness and tenderness, from which the matriarchal superego grows. Women turn to goddess images to reach something alive and feminine that is so missing or so eclipsed in our culture that the only way to find it again is to cast it upwards metaphorically as divinity. Ironically, however, these goddess images can be a way of killing off the feminine as well, reverting to a view of woman as simply an impersonal natural force. In goddess religion woman is female sex, woman is blood, woman is fertility, woman is milk. We thus skip over or obliterate 2,000 years of woman established as an individual, a particular soul, a person. The symbolism and the pre-oedipal psychological dynamics of goddess imagery lead to merger of self and instinct, self and other, self and deity. Fusion is not union and loss of self differs radically from offering God the self one is and has. Women do not want to be reduced to a force of nature. Women want to be themselves, each one as she is, different, individual, greeted and cherished for herself and with that treatment joined to the whole human species.

Still, the potent appeal of goddess imagery symbolizes
a pressing theological need of our time, for a faith that
connects to where we live—to our dreams and to our ail-
ments, to our group life and to our work. In true
mediatrix fashion, women asking about the missing
feminine carry the burgeoning and unvoiced questions of
all of us that ask for a God connected to where we live,
that ask for a way to live close to the fire where all the
parts of us can be housed. Women pressing to draw into
themselves the missing feminine symbolize the pressing
of concrete claims by many groups in our time that want
to make God into their color, their social class, their political or sexual persuasion.[13] The woman's question is a
question we all are asking: What about our God-images
in relation to God? The feminine mode is connection,
linking. It asks about connection; it makes conscious in
all of us our deep desire for connection.

True to the down-going way of the feminine modality,
the woman's temptation is the temptation of all of us, a
specifically theological and spiritual one. We shift our
focus; we turn away. We no longer ask of God, Who are
you? Instead, we ask only, Who are you for me? Who are
you for my group? How can you empower our cause? As
children we asked God to let our team win. Although our
causes may be more sophisticated now—we want our
version of how to use nuclear power to win, our version
of justice to triumph—the psychological move is just the
same. As adults we want our pictures of God to be God.
They catch us, just as the serpent caught Eve. What was
only a picture now becomes the real thing. What was
merely a symbol now becomes a symbolic equation. God
now is Marxist; God now is archetype; God now is goddess, black, mother, sister, brother. We have not housed
the image; we have identified with it. And what we have

not housed we are pushing our neighbor to house for us. Thus we perpetuate a theological sadism as vicious as any visited upon our ancestors in the past. For God is now to be used to buttress our vision of reality. We forget how much we are like the woman with all the parts of her life gathered together except for the deep emptiness at the center, which she felt she had to stuff with food. We forget how much we hunger and what we really hunger for.

I want to press the issue further. For here is an instance of the last becoming first. The woman's question—the question we women are asking of religious tradition is leading us to the edge of something new. Again, let me begin with something small, again with a dream. The dreamer is a woman, well established in her profession, but still suffering terrible attacks in which she feels reduced to something trivial, altogether negligible as compared with the masculine. She feels if a man speaks at a professional meeting, what he says must always be wise and profound; if she speaks, what she says is "trivial, shallow, and obvious." Her dream gave her great hope. She dreamt of a woman she admired and had learned a great deal from. The woman comes and sits herself down in front of the dreamer, in a way that retains a lot of space behind her back. She says to the dreamer: "I'm sitting this way because I know that the Spirit comes into me from the back. From where does the Spirit come into you?" That question changed the woman's problem. It was the leaven that transformed the whole issue. The dream focused on her feminine connection to the Spirit. That was the point, not how she compared with her masculine colleagues. In psychodynamic terms, she split off and projected onto men this connecting link to the Spirit and inflated their insight with her own unlived penetration. But the dream gives the quicker route. It goes directly to the substantive question—Where does the Spirit enter you?—which is more direct than any interpretation, however flexible and open to mutations.

This intensely personal question for the dreamer voices a question many are asking today. Where does the Spirit come into me, not, who has more and who has less? How does the Spirit come *into* us, really into us? How does it come into our body, from the back or the front? How does the Spirit enter our flesh, that concreteness that is not just an idea, but also an experience, that is not just an objéct of knowledge, but also a way of the soul? How does the Spirit come into the body of our church? The body of our society? The groups we belong to? It is the intensity of our wanting to know that which tempts us to be like God, to think we can know what God is, to identify with our God-image.

We need woman's wiles instead of this identification. We need the indirect route, not a blunt equation. We need that special mediating presence to house all these personal and group god-images and bring them to God. The Spirit comes to us in our receiving of it and giving birth to it into the world, out of the enwombing housing of our lives. This is wisdom as female and the female as wisdom.

III.

Finally, I am coming into deep waters to talk about the Trinity, an image central to the Episcopalian tradition. We recite the Trinitarian formula in our morning and evening prayers, as part of every blessing. It begins our credal statement. The Trinity can be likened to the big house of God, the great tent in which God dwells. As I said before, it is an audacious image. It is daring to describe what God is doing when God is in fact not doing a thing. It describes God's "self," not our experience of God or how God is to us, but rather God when God is just being. In psychoanalytic terms it is as if the Trinity were a means of describing the inner object-relations of God, God's true self, or God's ego-self connection.[14] That inner life is paradoxical; its essence is relationship, and endlessly circulating love, given out totally, taken in totally, given back again. It is a circulating love so palpable, so tangible, that the love itself possesses its own shape and personhood. What goes on there is a constant giving, receiving, and giving back, all interdependent and all connected— an autonomy of connectedness independent of, but not unrelated to us.[15] We are invited into this tent, into this big house, into its circulating currents. It seeks us to come into us, to take up residence in us.

Here we find the theological meaning of women's questions about the missing feminine. In asking where the feminine is in the Trinity, we are asking where is our connection with the Godhead, where does our experience count? The woman's question carries with it—and mediates to consciousness—the question we are all always asking: What about me? About us? What have you, God, to do with my particular situation, color, country, my images of you? How do we house you who house us? And how do you house us who house you? Here, woman stands for all of us. She is the urge to make connection, a connection more palpable than logical, much more in a setting than abstracted from it, touching more than analyzed, felt and thought rather than studied. We need both modes of perception, but one is missing and left behind as last. Now it becomes first. For symbolized in

woman's question *and* in her wiles, her beguilement with
what is, is her great gaping need for connection, even in
and to the Godhead.

This question about the missing feminine, with all its
symbolic impact, has been left behind in history until
very late. It has never been asked this way before. Other
questions were asked, but never this one this way. This
full range was missing. This was the lost mite, the little
thing. You remember all those wonderful questions,
those heartfelt ones that took you right into the intimacy
of God's life? How could God be creator and sovereign
and yet suffer? How could Jesus be born and die and still
be God? How can there be three parts to God and God
still be one? How are the three related? Are they equal?
Are they from the same or from a different substance? Do
they come out of each other? All these questions—of
unity, diversity, substance, relation, divinity, equality,
persons, processions—are fascinating and wonderful
questions. But see, not one question is asked about the
female or the feminine. That was unimportant, we used
to think, a little thing, a lost mite. But now we scour the
whole house to find it.

Something new begins, voiced in this woman's question. We have come to a point where something new
might happen there at the center of all being. We hear a
different voice. We have a different vision. Hence, we are
temptable and held by some to be contemptible. A differentiation has occurred. We are not mankind, we are
man- and womankind. We are not humanity. We are
women and men. And we are all different in our sameness. What is voiced is the new possibility that in woman
is also man; and in man, also woman. Each is both. We
have a feminine and masculine mode within each of us.
When we add the feminine, the whole changes. What we

perceive is the new possibility of contrasexuality where a man knows the missing feminine as a part of himself he needs to find; woman's wiles are of all things his! A woman looks to house the masculine in herself as belonging to her own feminine personality, not just to be fought or admired in the men around her. Because we can ask about the missing feminine, we perceive we are no longer one lump of humanity, but now different persons faced with the same task, to put the masculine and feminine parts together and try to find out how they have or have not gone together all along. This task faces us all, old, young, heterosexual, homosexual, lesbian, celibate, coupled, married, single. Reversion to matriarchy only excludes the masculine; fixation on patriarchy only cuts out the feminine. Because we can now ask about how the feminine goes together with the Godhead described as the Trinity, we perceive we are also asking how feminine and masculine modes of being connect within our own psyches and souls, and how each of us with both modes connects with each other and how together as a people we live in the tent of God. The connections are triple, trinitarian. The links within our interior lives are of the feminine and masculine modes of being, the connections between men and women who know their own contrasexuality, the movements showing us how any and all of us move toward union with God.

Like any new perception breaking into consciousness it backs into place, full of clumsiness, imprecise language, general mess, and upheaval. I think we must just live with all of that, with its ambiguity and its struggle, and try not to tidy it up too fast. We must not jump over the missing feminine to embrace the appealing image of androgyny, an identity beyond male and female. What kind of solution can that be? The feminine has been neglected for centuries, and now it is not to matter any more; we are beyond it. There must be a time—and I think ours is the time, with all our anger and hurt, with all our raised fists and our open palms—when the feminine can have its chance to be herself, her many selves, together and differently. We must acknowledge the threat within us that we attribute to the opposite sex and struggle to house it and realize that struggle is also our struggle to relate to God. Through the neglected other within us, the Divine Other breaks in.

From this perspective, we can see the symbolic meanings and shortcomings of the various revisions of the trinitarian doctrine with which some propose to answer the question about the missing feminine. Others throw the Trinity out altogether. The symbol has lost its symbolic power, we are told, is now a mere sign, and worse, a sign of negativity, of male oppression and bigotry. In this argument, the Trinity is a sign of the exclusion of the feminine, an emblem of its missing state, both in language and iconography. That very trinitarian symbol now bespeaks woman's pain, anger, and oppression. Therefore it must be thrown out, and the pain, anger, and oppression brought in as the new departure point. Woman's experience of marginalization and discrimination will become the new hermeneutic starting-point from which to do theology and correct the anthropocentric bias of tradition. This view has its worthy side. It brings pain right back where it belongs, in the midst of theological systems. The problem with this route, however, is that what begins as a cry of pain and anger, lifting a crushing stone from women's chests, must now constantly be recharged and refueled, not just to maintain group cohesion, but to secure and preserve the her-

meneutic starting-point. What begins as a freeing of
women from pain ends by imprisoning them in it.

Another revision removes the language of persons in
the Trinity to insert the language of function: Creator,
Redeemer, Comforter, to substitute for Father, Son, and
Holy Spirit. Here, too, the traditional image has lost its
symbolizing power. Two of the persons have come to
many to seem to be like an ordinary father and son and
one wonders where are the mother and daughter, while
the Spirit is left as a merely tangential, windy male
presence. This effort can be commendable, then, as we try
to break out of a symbol that has degenerated into a sign.
The problem remains, however: we get functions instead
of persons; impersonal, abstract terms describe opera-
tions, not relationship. A father who gives his son gives
his life into the world. A creator gives only a product.

Another problem with this route is its Chinese-menu
approach. You get God in Column A—the Creator creates.
The Redeemer does not create. The Redeemer sits in
Column B and redeems. The Sustainer performs a self-
defined function over in C. The original intuition about
the inner life of God in the Trinity recognizes that
everybody does everything. They "mutually inexist";
"And so each is in each, all are in each, each is in all, all
are in all, and all are one."[16] "Each Person of the Trinity
is God, and all together are one God. Each is the full essence, and all together are One essence."[17]

Both of these revisions miss the symbolic power of the
Trinity that points to the inner *life of God* in itself. They
reverse the order and put as a prior question how God's
life affects *me* and *us* and *my* life or *our* life. The Trinity of
tradition concentrates on the living reality of God as love-
in-relationship, a continuous unfolding and refolding in

which the Unknowable reveals itself, knowing itself, and returning back to itself.[18]

Still another revision of the traditional understanding of the Trinity is to make Mary one of the boys. Either she is really the Spirit, or she should be, or she should be added to the three as a missing fourth. Jung is very fond of this solution.[19] Again, the benefit is the distinct recognition that the feminine really is missing and is sorely missed. The problem in this version lies with its style of approach. It is a caricature of a masculine kind of fix-it procedure. It veers toward making theology into a set of engineering problems. These three are over here and then over there is a missing thing; so let's stick it in. This is a phallic style of problem-solving, rather than a feminine meditative style of brooding and pondering over a mystery. This is an amiable enough kind of additive solution, the feminine cheerfully added on, but it does not connect woman to the felt meaning of the Trinity, nor to the power of this symbol that conveys its interior energy, moving all women into its future unfolding. At best it is an intellectual solution. At worst it does not quicken the heart at all. And that is the point, isn't it, to quicken the heart, to connect it, again, to that central fire?

We need a woman's wiles to point the way. The woman's way will not clarify through discursive reasoning, nor through power tactics, but rather through its characteristic beguilement, curving round and down to the center, moving into the anguish, into the dread, into all that is startling and new, even if at the price of being tricked or tempted.

Women's questions about the missing feminine carry all our questions in these last decades of our century. Their anguish carries all of our anguish, where in our dread we are stripped of all defenses, standing in our

nothingness before God, without clear justification, utterly dependent on the gift of grace, where there is no link
to God except the one God gives us. In this place the ladder of our images stops, breaks off, breaks down. Even
the images God gives us fall away. The Trinity image itself does not cross the gap. As Augustine, that great lover
of the Trinity, said: "The Trinity . . . falls . . . very far short
of Him of whom we think, nor comprehends him as He
is; . . ."[20] And now, in this crisis, we know it, but it is not
enough to have this insight.

Women's wiles show us how to proceed, for the Trinity
image is at the heart of our liturgy and our theology. We
need connection to it if faith is to quicken the heart, and
we are to find a bridge across the gap between the present
and the past of tradition. Here I take a pointer from my
clinical profession, alerted to pay very close attention to
the image, to see if it gives any hint, any clue to the
desired answers. The Trinity enters the world through
Mary. She houses the Word sent by God, in which God
lives, He who will leave us the Comforter, the consoling
Spirit. The Trinity houses her as she houses it. It inhabits
her. It takes up residence in her. You remember those
wonderful statues of wood, the opening virgin (la Vièrge
Ouvrante), where the Virgin Mary on the outside sits
calm, even stony, but then opens to reveal inside the
Father, the Son on the cross, and the Spirit.

Are we, then, all of us, men and women alike, are *we*
the missing feminine? Are we the fourth in a Quaternity,
if you like, the earth in whom God plants the seed, as the
parable says? Are we, then, the house in which the Godhead finds its missing part? For when the Godhead joined
us, it made all of us a part of a feminized creation. It
entered woman, in whom all creation found its source,
not just as a friendly womb, but as a place to be. For what

is it that enters our humanity but that great tent of God?
God's own interior being, a being of endlessly circulating
love, of independence and interdependence. That house
of the Trinity with no boundaries, that house that can include everything and move itself anywhere—we are held
in that house and the house holds us. We are pulled into
its currents of circulating love. We are pierced by its being
flowing into the world. We pray that "We do not
presume" to come to the Eucharist except that we trust in
God's mercy, so that, taking the sacrament, "Christ may
dwell in us and we in him." In taking the Eucharist we
recover the sustaining truth that we are like Mary receiving God, a being penetrated and opened by God's indwelling that will then be borne through us into the
world. God comes into us before we come into God.
God's antecedent love makes our loving response part of
the eternal circulation of a divine outgoing, bestowing,
and giving back. This is being before doing; this is a being
that is at once a becoming.

We are called into the life in Christ, born of the spirit
through baptism in the font of Mary-as-Church to do
God's will in the world after God has first dwelt in Mary.
So does God dwell in us before we dwell in God. What
kind of God is this that is come into the world, born of
woman? This God does not link women with death but
with life in the world, with accessibility, with love. This
God is not kept safely immortal, altogether different from
us and untouched by us. This God enters the feminine as
the means of access, to come in person to the world. Are
we then, all of us as Mary, called repeatedly to receive the
overshadowing God, who would live in us, into the
world? Are we humans the four-cornered base of the
pyramid of the Trinity, that which earths it, thus making
us participate in the ongoing eternal incarnation?

We can even speculate that the imagery of God come into and born of woman without a human father symbolizes the way religious experience implants itself and gestates in us. It comes in and through the feminine mode of our being. It comes through the matrix of the unconscious, unfathered by any conscious skill, neither created nor authorized by any cultural intent or anything else that we could claim as our doing. It comes through the dark mothering unconscious of our being. It comes through the feminine as one-in-herself, as virgin, that capacity in us to receive the transcendent each time as for the first time. Mary also symbolizes the appropriate ego-attitude to such momentous happenings. She hears. She sees. She feels the impact, the mark. She feels unworthy and without understanding. She takes what is offered and receives into her being the great house of being. We then, as men and women in touch with our feminine mode of being, are the missing feminine in the Godhead. Receiving God's grace we join into God's life. The Trinity dwells among us. That is what happens to us when the fire burns in us. Think of people who have lived this love into the world, people in whose presence, whether they are male or female, you feel the capacity to be born.

I think of a woman in Harlem who has been written and talked about in New York quite a bit the last few years. For forty years now, after finishing her raising of her own children, she has been taking into her home the infants of drug-addicted prostitutes. She is now in her eighties and very well known in Harlem. Women come and leave their babies on her doorstep. The babies they bring are addicted. She does not treat them with drugs, which is the usual medical way with children. She said in one interview: "I love them back into being." That means holding the infants and walking up and down with them,

singing and talking to them as they suffer withdrawal
from the drugs. If the babies are made well, and the
mothers have kicked their own habits, she gives the
babies back to their mothers. Recently, she has added to
her family babies afflicted with AIDS. There in her, is the
love we have been talking about, love pulled into the
world, love brought almost violently back into circulation.

I think too of a former student of mine who as a young
chaplain was the only one to sit with a deformed and
dying baby, to baptize it. The parents were too shocked
even to hold their baby. Doctors could do nothing more
for the baby. So there she was with a dying infant, bringing the infant into the house of God and witnessing the
house of God taking up residence in the dying infant.

Another witness, a parish priest, offers space in the
church community's life to a woman who feels and acts
crazy because she is afflicted with schizophrenia. She will
not be treated psychiatrically. Her family can do nothing
with her. The priest can. He invites her into the church's
life while at the same time refusing to put up with the
wildest of her performances. He treats her as a human
being called to house God's being even as God's being
houses her. She is allowed to be in charge of posting the
numbers of hymns to be sung in church services. When
she decides to post the wrong numbers, or repeatedly
posts only the numbers of her favorite hymns, or worse
still refuses to post any numbers at all, the priest steps in
with a firm hand. They engage in a power struggle, which
he, *with luck*, wins because she knows that there in this
church there is a home for her.

This circulation of love for which we may be the house
forces us to step out into the unknown, to leave the

familiar, as Abraham did—whether it be for job, relation-ship, marriage, country, whatever. It moves us to take the good offered us, to hold tight to the images God gives us, only suddenly to be surprised when at the next moment God smashes those same images. The missing feminine is the connecting link between a faith professed and a faith lived. It gives us the wiles to live next to the gap. It brings something new into the ministry, not just females doing male jobs, but females bringing something different of their own, speaking in their own voice, offering up their own way of hearing, their own way of receiving God.

What opens us then to receive this offering of being is the feminine within us, within us women, within us men. What crosses the gap from God's side is love. Nothing in the abstract; all in the flesh. For what we seek is not a solu-tion so much as a conjunction, not a perfect explanation, but something like completion, an inhabiting of God's house, knowledge about it. God comes; we open. God opens; we go in. As housekeepers, then, let us live in this love, ready for it, housing it, being housed by it, allowing the gap to be crossed from God's side.

NOTES

1. For description of the archetypal figure of the witch, see Ann and Barry Ulanov, *The Witch and the Clown: Two Archetypes of Human Sexuality* (Wilmette: Chiron, 1987), chapter 2.
2. Ann and Barry Ulanov, *Religion and the Unconscious*, pp. 153–154. For discussion of the feminine mode of being, see Ann Belford Ulanov, *The Feminine in Jungian Psychology and in Christian Theology* (Evanston: North-western University Press, 1971), chapters 8 and 9.

3. See Ann and Barry Ulanov, "The Hag: Wise Woman Manquée," in *The Witch and the Clown*.

4. In a fascinating and funny chapter, Paul Roazen describes the brilliant women who surrounded Freud and developed his theories further, See Paul Roazen, *Freud and His Followers* (New York: Alfred A. Knopf, 1975), chapter IX. Much as with Freud, a large number of the early followers of Jung were women.

5. See C. G. Jung, "Psychological Aspects of the Mother Archetype," in *The Archetypes of the Collective Unconscious, Collected Works*, Vol. 9:1, trans. R.F.C. Hull (New York: Pantheon, 1959); see also Melanie Klein, *Love, Guilt and Reparation and Other Works 1921–1945*, pp. 42, 173, 190–191, 195, 202, 224, 237, 244, 276, 281–282, 345, 375, 393, 405, and 413; see also D. W. Winnicott, *Through Paediatries to Psycho-Analysis* (New York: Basic Books, 1975), p. 99; see also D. W. Winnicott, *Babies and Their Mothers* (Reading, MA: Addison-Wesley, 1987), chapter 1.

6. See Heinz Kohut, *The Analysis of the Self* (New York: International Universities Press, 1971), and *The Restoration of the Self* (New York: International Universities Press, 1977); see also Otto Kernberg, *Borderline Conditions and Pathological Narcissism* (New York: Jason Aronson, 1975).

7. For a detailed discussion of these modes of being, see Ann Belford Ulanov, *Receiving Woman, Studies in the Psychology and Theology of the Feminine* (Philadelphia: Westminster Press, 1981), pp. 76–80.

8. See Ann Belford Ulanov, *The Feminine*, chapter 9.

9. Falling into a symbolic equation is a normal phase in the development of a capacity for symbolization. Trouble looms if we get stuck there, where word and thing are both equated and confused with self. The

separation that allows one simply to stand for the other has not yet occurred. For example, we understand our wrist watch not as representing or pointing to time, but as actually to *be* time. Then, if we smash our watch, we believe we have smashed time itself. We are caught in a delusion. A symbol, in contrast, both makes space and constricts links to objects across space. The face of our watch configures the invisibility of time, bringing us conceptions of it or images of its reality while simultaneously confirming its transcendence beyond all our conceptions and images. A symbol separates self and object so that one can stand for the other. Then we can tolerate the quite separate identities of self and object, and bridge our inner and outer worlds. Thus it is that a symbol puts us in touch with our unconscious. We gain much when we use symbols this way—awareness of the ambivalence of our emotions, impulses, and fantasies, and new opportunities to integrate them with reality. Through symbols we discover opportunities to make reparation for destructiveness, not only our own, but that of others. David Holbrook contrasts manic and schizoid symbolism with what he calls creative symbolism. David Holbrook, *Human Hope and the Death Instinct* (Oxford: Pergamon Press, 1971), chapters 17 and 19. See also David Holbrook, *The Masks of Hate* (Oxford: Pergamon, 1972), chapters 26 and 27.

10. I have also discussed these dangers that arise from identification with our images in "Picturing God," in the book of that name, pp. 169–171.

11. For discussions of these alternative paths see Carol P. Christ, "Symbols of Goddess and God in Feminist Theology," in *The Book of the Goddess*, ed. Carl Olsen (New York: Crossroads, 1983); see also Caroline

Walker Bynum, *Jesus as Mother, Studies in the Spirituality of the High Middle Ages* (Berkeley: University of California Press, 1982).

12. A full dream interpretation here would need to reach to the reverse possibility as well, seeing that church duties may also be a means of repressing the dangerous sexuality symbolized by the journalist's escapade. Dreams are multi-valent. Which interpretation actually obtains in the present moment depends on the patient's associations and response, in other words, what clicks.

13. We can also understand this pull to particularity as a beginning of differentiation of subjectivity through issues and elements associated with categories such as race, color, sex, culture, and class.

14. R. C. Zaehner points out that the image of the Trinity distinguishes Christian monotheism from the other great monotheisms of the world, those of Islam and Judaism, because in the Trinity oneness dwells in relationship, with a begetting, a begottenness, and a loving bond of union between them. See R. C. Zaehner, "The Holy and Undivided Trinity," in *The City Within the Heart* (New York: Crossroad, 1981). See also Leonard Hodgson, *The Doctrine of the Trinity* (London: Nisbet, 1943), pp. 105, 183.

15. The Anglican theologian Philip Turner writes, "The doctrine of the Trinity places presence and exchange at the heart of the inner life of God. It is of God's eternal nature to bestow all he is and receive back all he has given. The traditional way of saying this is, "God is love." Turner continues, "God lives and is love because presence, bestowal, and counter-bestowal lie eternally at the heart of his life." Philip Turner, *Sex,*

Money and Power (Cambridge: Cowley Publications, 1985), p. 19.

See also Edmund J. Fortman's summary of Augustine on the nature of the relations of the Persons in the Trinity: "Augustine does not say that the Persons *are* relations, but rather that they are distinguished from one another by their unchangeable relations to one another (paternity, filiation, gift). Edmund J. Fortman, *The Triune God, A Historical Study of the Doctrine of the Trinity* (Philadelphia: Westminster Press, 1972), p. 144.

See also John Thurmer, *A Detection of the Trinity* (Exeter: Paternoster Press, 1984) where he gives various examples of the relations in the Trinity among three who are one. Some of them are: God as Father is thought, Son is act, Spirit is perceiving the act in recollection; Father is music in the mind of the composer, Son is music, Spirit is a reading of the scores which renew the music; Father is lover, Son is beloved, Spirit is the love which binds them; Father is idea, Son is creative energy, Spirit is creative power and meaning and the response of the soul; Father is inner self, Son is revealed self, Spirit is effective self which others see and understand; Father is idea, Son is activity; Spirit is the power which flows back from activity to the authoring idea.

16. Augustine, *De Trinitate* 6.10.12, cited by Fortman, *op. cit.*, p. 141.
17. Augustine, *De Doctrina Christiana* 1.5, cited by Fortman, p. 141. Augustine searched also for analogies to the Trinity in human personality. Lover, beloved, and the love between them is one of his more famous triads. His favorite was memory (more like anamnesis than history- taking, a recollection of who we are in

our truest selves), understanding, and will (more like willingness to respond wholeheartedly than will-power). Augustine, *On the Trinity*, trans. A. W. Haddan (Edinburgh: T. & T. Clark, 1873), 10.11, 17–19, pp. 258–260.

18. Fortman quotes Hymn 3 of Victorinus, saying he sees God "as in a continuous process of unfolding and re-folding." The hymn: "O blessed Trinity . . . In sub-stance Thou art God, in form Word, in knowledge Holy Spirit; Being, Life, Knowledge; Fixity, Progress, Regress; First Entity, Second Entity, Third Entity; Yet the three but one. Word, God, the Holy Spirit, Thou art the same, O blessed Trinity. Thou, Holy Spirit, art the connecting link . . . Thou dost first link Two, and art Thyself the Third. . . ." Fortman, *op. cit.*, p. 136.

19. See C. G. Jung, *Psychology and Religion* in *Psychology and Religion: West and East*, pp. 52, 63, 71–73; pars. 91, 107, 123–126, See also C. G. Jung, "A Psychological Ap-proach to the Dogma of the Trinity," in *Psychology and Religion: West and East*, pp. 161, 164–175, 189, pars. 240, 243–259, 281.

See also Deborah Belonick, "The Spirit of Female Priesthood," in *Women and the Priesthood*, ed. Thomas Hopko (Crestwood, New York: St. Vladimir's Semi-nary Press, 1983); see also Jean Gebser, *The Ever-Present Origin*, trans. Noel Barstad with Algis Mickunas (Athens: Ohio University Press, 1984), pp. 229–236.

20. Augustine, *On the Trinity*, 5.1.1., p. 145. Nonetheless, Augustine closes in his long study of the Trinity with an ardent prayer that begins, "O Lord God, we believe in Thee, the Father, the Son and the Holy Spirit." He concludes: ". . . the wise man spake of Thee in his book . . . . Ecclesiasticus, 'We speak,' he said, 'Much, and yet

come short; and in sum of words, He is all.' And we shall say one thing without end, in praising Thee in one, ourselves also made one in Thee. 0 Lord the one God, God the Trinity. . . ." *Ibid.*, 15.38.51, pp. 438–439.

Meister Eckhart and Karl Barth offer supporting and contrasting views. Like Augustine, who recognizes that even the image of the Trinity cannot be equated with God, Eckhart differentiates the Father, Son, and Spirit, whom he calls God, from the nameless unity and silence of Being, which he calls the Godhead. *Meister Eckhart*, trans. Raymond B. Blakney (New York: Harper & Brothers, 1941), Sermons 1 and 16, See also Louis Dupré, *The Deeper Life, An Introduction to Christian Mysticism* (New York: Crossroads, 1981), pp. 44 ff., pp. 48–49.

In contrast, Barth takes the Trinity as rooted in God's revelation. The doctrine of the Trinity is "a work of the Church," but it is "a necessary and relevant analysis of revelation." Hence God's three-in-oneness is a way we talk about God's self-disclosure. Fortman, *op. cit.*, p. 260.

THE WISDOM OF THE PSYCHE

I.

In the previous chapters I have examined the wisdom of the psyche under three rubrics: the ego and its task to house what we've been given to be; our confrontations with good and evil—our shadow issues; and our need for conscious connection to the feminine mode of being to meet our ego tasks, to claim the good, and to energize us in our struggle with evil. What follows here must follow, I think, a view of how and where the psyche establishes its place in the religious scheme of things.

Work with the psyche must go further than unshackling its resources for a fuller life. That unshackling is no small thing in itself, as all of us can testify who have suffered bondage to compulsion and achieved release from it through psychological work. Whether our addiction fastens on a work schedule, a regimen of neatness, a bedtime ritual, a diet program, on drink, drugs, or sexual obsession, we know the humiliation and degradation that accompanies such a slavish state of being. It is like living under totalitarian regimes, St. Paul's principalities and powers. We know too the sweeping gratitude that floods us when we are liberated from such bondage by a greater power. Even though we have worked at our psyche in painstaking, laborious ways, sometimes for many years, we know deep down in ourselves that the work, though necessary, was not sufficient. Liberation when it comes is a gift, something inexplicable that breaks in upon us. Though related to our work, it does not seem to be de-

pendent on it nor to be caused by it. The relation of our
human efforts to this in-breaking of releasing power
remains mysterious, awesome. To say, then, that the
psyche and psychoanalytical work can perform the work
of unshackling us, freeing us to live what we have been
given, is not to say something inconsequential. It is to say
a great deal. But we must go further still, to assert in ways
of psychic life those things which are permanent and
wise, to go beyond the dropping of the chains of the
psyche to the taking up of the joys of the freedom of the
spirit.

Many of the insights given us in and through the
psyche point to that something in the human psyche
which is lasting, where the psyche unmistakably reflects
the spirit. In our collective life, where we work to transform collectivity into community, some of the spiritual
character of the ego-self life of individuals necessarily
reproduces itself, because the collective is made up of individuals, many of whom possess that spirituality at
some stage of development.[1] In fact, one of the necessary
steps in transforming bunches of people, mere collectivities, into groups of people living in relation to each
other as communities, is precisely the recognition that we
share as individuals the same kind of life, both of psyche
and of spirit. We recognize self-in-other, the domain of
spirit, and we experience its claims to which our own
egos must respond, and for which sometimes we even
must make sacrifices. The insistent strength of the psyche
points to the spirit, not to be diminished by it, certainly
not to be eclipsed by it, but that both may be enhanced in
the meeting.

My view differs here from others who tackle this
problematic, this identification of the ground of psyche
in the religious scheme of things. Some who have thought

about this want to explain away religion by translating it into psychological terms, entirely reducing the epistemology of spirit to that of the psyche.[2] In so doing, they leave out the flesh of the matter. The concrete living of the spiritual life, in terms of worship, community, rituals of prayer and service, are subsumed in the language and process of psychological ritual. It is a strong and a tempting argument, for those rituals are necessary, urgent indeed to all who take their psyche's existence seriously. But they are not complete in themselves and never can be. To work with dreams, for example, to meditate on their meaning and try to fold that meaning into the heavy stuff of one's daily life, is a process as delicate and decisive for the outcome of the whole as folding stiff, aerated egg whites into a souffle'; it is a task requiring practice, finesse, and luck. If it works, it develops in us the life of the spirit, our capacity to commune with the unseen. But it is not the same as, nor does it even substitute for the most crude and childish efforts to pray to the source of unseen reality, which is to say, the source of psyche.

The audacious work of religion is to try to establish personal relation to the center. The center is that which not only acknowledges our small selves but loves and cherishes them. Wisdom is the product of a lasting *sapientia*, not of an ephemeral *scientia*. Depth psychology concerns itself with *scientia*, the world of transitory things where we live so much of our lives, but that world cannot fill us for long unless it prepares us for and leads us to spiritual understanding, to the realm of *sapientia*. Analysis leads to, points toward, the transcendent.[3] Failure to acknowledge that function is one strong reason analysis often fails to work and why analytical groups are so often full up with controversies and petty squabbles even when they are very creative. I think, for example, of the British Psychoanalytical Society which fought for two decades over the merits of the theories of Melanie Klein and Anna Freud, while a middle group of analysts, people like D. W. Winnicott, Marion Milner, and Michael Balint, grew up outside the quarrel, rich in its own creativity, alive in its own spirit.[4]

All analytical theories reach toward the transcendent; few explicitly acknowledge its existence, and even those usually do so hesitantly, nervously. Hence the ultimate, not pointed to, all but outlawed, falls into the unconscious, expressing itself in the fervor with which factions defend their theories, each time as if truth itself, ultimate truth, were at stake. Those who disagree are put to a stake of sorts, exiled to peripheral status, sometimes marked taboo, and what remains is endless haggling and haranguing.[5] The failure to acknowledge explicitly the transcendent element in theories of the psyche inevitably leads to such fanaticism. It is, as we know too well, the same in the church, though the virulence comes from the opposite end. There people do explicitly acknowledge the transcendent, but they easily skip over its impact on the psyche, its effect on our reception of the transcendent into our daily life. It does not get acknowledged all the way down into our unconscious lives, where it must find its place, in our sexuality, in our aggression. So in the church too people get stuck in the identifying of the ultimate with the pointers to it and new fanaticisms spring up.

At the end of the spectrum of theory about the role of the psyche in a religious view of things where the psyche becomes all, it turns into a great dumping place, a lowest common denominator to which all religious expressions can be reduced. The result is a religiosity about matters psychological with an aggressive showing of intolerance, with holier-than-thou rhetoric, fanatic zeal in support of the position and outright persecution of opponents.

We see here the danger of a young discipline. Depth psychology is barely a century old. It is not only young, it is often primitive in its attitudes and procedures. It contains, both in its subject-matter and its way of dealing with it, a lot of crude raw life. It is an exciting world, even at its most raw, perhaps especially then. When people get involved in it, they are gripped, fascinated, tempted to take parts for wholes. It offers one of the most alluring of the utopian diversions: everyone should be analyzed; then the world will become safe. All that is needed to explode that theory is to become an analyst, and survive in the field for twenty years or more, to go to analytic meetings and join with other analysts who have been analyzed and find oneself still caught up in fighting, pettiness, in inanities of empty discussion, and procedural imbroglios, all mixed up at the same time with genuine research, deeply satisfying professional conversation and the marvelous hard work involved in the search for better ways to understand and treat the human psyche.

On the other side of this theoretical spectrum are the people, also deeply interested in matters psychological and religious, who do the opposite, who collapse the psyche into the spirit, usually defined in the full detail of their own religious denomination. What they usually ignore completely is the actual existence of the unconscious, the fact of its existence and its particular life in each of us.[6] It is thought all right here to investigate ethical metaphors, to identify and survey the metaphysical horizons of a given school of depth psychology, but the aim almost always is to restrict, indeed to jump over, the extraordinary life of the psyche, the world of the uncon-

scious, not only in each of us as individuals but among
us in groups as well, in our collectivities and communities. What is ignored or misidentified is the force of
psychic energy which runs through our cultural, political, and economic systems.[7] Sometimes these critics take
a particularly sociological tone, proclaiming that what is
needed is social-systems analysis, not psychoanalysis, to
address all the many pressing problems of today's world.
The question I always want to ask is, Why the "either/or"
approach? Why not, "both/and"? Social-systems
analysis has its value but it is no substitute for work with
the psyche. One discipline cannot be collapsed into the
other without both falling apart. A gap properly exists between them. Their differences inform and stimulate research, knowledge, dialogue, every sort of discovery of
what lies below the surface of things. There can be a
tyranny of mental health too. Depth psychology is no
substitute for political action or social analysis, but I
would argue strongly it must be included in those ven-
tures. It is not yet included enough in social awareness
nor in theological curriculums. But the balance tips more
heavily toward doing social analysis, partly because
depth psychology is still a young discipline, but mainly
because people are afraid to acknowledge their own
psyches. This means recognizing energies, impulses, fantasies, needs working *in us* and in all our social dealings
that we do not know about and do not control. That requires courage of the first order, a great deal of persistent, unobtrusive work on oneself that does not get
headlines but that changes the social situation from the
inside out, the way the discovery of underground springs
waters and makes fertile the ground so that things grow.
Any effort to use analysis to avoid social issues and in-
volvement fails. It will not work. The analysis will be

fake. The self in its very essence is social and the work we do on ourselves will push us into social congress.

At this religious end of the spectrum, the tough facts of the psyche are skipped over—the rude confronting images our unconscious tosses up to us in nightly dreams, the brute energy of archetype and instinct that stands against good intentions and reasonable expectations—all in aid of the construction of intellectual schemas showing how depth psychology goes with religion. But what a loss—the great impact of the lived psyche, the experience of the unconscious breaking in upon us, sometimes to bless, sometimes to wound. Dreams can terrify. A woman dreamt that she came home to her apartment to find her front door bulging outward, "as if it was going to blow up. A fierce buzzing sound came from within my home. I knew that flies, bees, hornets were swarming there and I couldn't go in there anymore." Six months later the dreamer was diagnosed as suffering from a terminal malignant brain tumor. Dreams can also bless, by putting us in touch with lost parts of ourselves, newly found; by touching us deeply with the sheer beauty of being; by putting before us a numinous scene. One woman dreamt that in cleaning out the attic closet she had discovered a whole new room hiding inside it. There she found "many treasures, an old diamond pin, a wooden relic of a saint and all the old doll house furniture," a world of things priceless to her as a little girl. There was more: "A big wolfish dog, whom I pet; I feel its fur. . . ." Still another woman dreamt she was invited to be the guest at a large house in the middle of the city. "In its big marble foyer near the outdoors are large open beds of peony flowers, hundreds of them, gorgeous pale pinks, roses, and whites. I hear them opening in the dream." A fourth woman dreamt that she was traveling in a foreign land. From her small hotel room, on a stone cliff, she looked with her lover down on land. There is a great forest, right at the center of town, a deep green one with high trees. "Through the green, you look down into its dark interior. The center of town is a marketplace, old and spacious and full of the activity of the people who live there. A river runs through the town center too. In front of the forest is a huge ornately carved wooden facade, almost like a rood screen one sees before the altar in old churches. It is an awesome scene. It is as if everything comes together at the center—water and forest, human activity and nature, and a symbol of the unseen mystery that authors it all."

Instead of including such experience in one's speculating at this end of the spectrum, people talk *about* the unconscious while avoiding the fact of it, its actual lived life. The result may be an interesting intellectual system, but such speculations function to deny and to defend against the reality of the psyche. That is dangerous, just as dangerous as denying and avoiding the transcendent. More precisely, it is another way to avoid the transcendent as it speaks to us out of our depths, through the things of which we are ordinarily unconscious.

We might sum up the problems of these two opposing views of the relation of depth psychology to religion by saying to begin with that depth psychology in its focus on subjective experience does not ask explicitly whether our experience of the transcendent points to something real and true, that actually exists. As a result, the feeling for the transcendent must express itself negatively, by an insistence on the correctness of one's theory or method of treatment, or training procedures for new analysts. A creeping rigidity develops, one that belies the very spirit at the heart of depth psychology, a spirit that is, or at least can be, flexibly respectful of human oddities and foibles, that honors the unique in the general, wherever and however it appears. By failing to acknowledge the transcendent dimension explicitly, by name, the flexible, respectful spirit stiffens. What follows is overemphasis on the general. An ersatz transcendent principle is articulated and in its own sorry way, it triumphs despite strong opposition. It issues forth in an increasingly didactic note in the enunciation of theory. Thus we hear from Freud that all women suffer penis envy—period. All men suffer castration anxiety—*gewiss*. All people go through precise and altogether nameable developmental stages. This last is a splendid way to inflict on fellow analysts, on trainees, on patients, on readers, a great sense of inferiority because one or another is invariably behind, stuck at an earlier stage, having failed to complete one particular stage or to graduate to the next. One poignant example comes from Jung's theories, the decisive experience of the self, that center of the whole psyche. It must always come in the image of a mandala, we are told. What if one never has had such an image? Too bad; no self-experience there. Or, as a patient of mine once said years ago, he was afraid with a previous analyst of not being a good enough patient, because he did not have quantities of "big" dreams, ones full of archetypal motifs, but only brought his doctor "little" dreams about his daily life.

I am not criticizing Freud and Jung here but rather trying to point out our obvious human propensity to sin. When we turn away from the transcendent, it does not go away; it just reappears in disguised form. We are apt to make gods out of our theories. What then of the true transcendent? When will it come to us? How?

Theology falls into the soup from the opposite side of the bowl. In its focus on the objective existence and na-

ture of God it leaves out the psyche's experience of God,
how the real affects us, what the psyche has to tell us in
our conscious formulations about the fact and nature of
God. It may fail then to make direct connection and the
Living Word may become just words, lively symbols perhaps but dead signs. That is terribly serious.[8] One
wonders at Judgement Day if teachers and preachers of
religion will not hear the thundering question, "Why did
you take something so alive, so burning with consuming
holy fire, and make it so dull, so dead?!"

We live in *the* psychological century, where explora-
tions of inner space probe as far as those that go into outer
space. Theology and the church hobble themselves when
they fail to recognize the broad deep rich life of the unconscious already there in religious ritual, symbol,
doctrine, and sacrament. It is a failure to take seriously
the transcendent in its persistent immanence, in and
among us. Within the system of the psyche, we experience unconscious contents as transcendent to our
egos. But if we accept the fact of the unconscious as existing here with us, even if unconsciously, we reach to a
sense of the transcendent that is beyond the whole
psyche, not just outside our egos. It does, however, make
itself known through the psyche, indeed, in each of its
most intimate personal elements and experiences, both of
personal and communal life.

Our experiences of the transcendent are amazing, as it
crosses the old boundaries of outside and inside, of the
God up there and us down here, those ancient separations
of transcendence and immanence, understood for so long
as conflicting opposites. To know them in direct experience is to know them interwoven with each other. The
opposite of both is reductionism, whether that of the
psychologist or the theologian or any other. Depth

psychology at its worst reduces in an upward spiral to formulas and concepts that do not persuade us because they do not inhere in us. Theology's failure to take the unconscious seriously leaves the immanence of God unreceived, unincarnated. Consciousness of the psyche's reception of God is essential if we are to perform the ministry of the ego in housing all that we are given to be. To reduce depth psychology to intellectual concepts that can be mapped and ranked and then found wanting because they do not concur with our preordained theological concepts is really to run away, to evade the full, big life that opens when one acknowledges the unconscious.[9] What we do this way is to put the unconscious in a box and then quickly shut the lid.

What would it mean not to fall into either of these polarized extremes? It would mean living with the gap between depth psychology and religion, not insisting that it be closed, but rather accepting that opening as a source of endless unfinishedness, knowing that one's theories will never finally close or cross the gap, understanding that the two disciplines will never entirely meet or agree. It would mean living with a radical openness to the transcendent that could overturn many of our theories, our theological symbols, our church programs, our prayer methods, our dream interpretations, to all of which we have become so deeply committed. The transcendent in its free entry into our lives could break in from above or below, overturning our psychological theories and our theological ones or extending or deepening them. We would be living consciously now with a keen sense of our dependence on the unconscious and the unknown, accepting the fact that we know a lot but recognizing too how much we do not know and can never know.

When at the beginning of this book I said that depth
psychology brings a new hermeneutic to theology, I
meant just this sort of new attitude at least as much as I
did the interpretive device of inquiring into the
psychological meaning of religious doctrine, symbol, and
text. The new attitude is central as it involves consciously making room for the unconscious in all our treatments
of God. It carries with it a bolder, a more conscious facing
of the fact that in all our theological formulations we
speak "as if" what we say were true. We never *know* for
certain. Every certainty is colored by our subjectivity and
our psychological experience of the spirit, large or small.
Consciously acknowledging that means always waiting
in the midst of speaking and acting, attending to what the
other side may say or do to announce itself.

At the same time, dogma, doctrine, and the symbols of
tradition remain the sure lines to which we can hold in
our acts of expectancy. We neither ignore the unconscious
nor deify it. We accept its existence right there in the
midst of what we take in consciously. In our acceptance
of the unconscious, and through the unconscious itself,
come images and affects, clues and reverberations of the
other side that complement, correct, and confound our
conscious images. We come, with whatever uncertainty,
to the other side. We learn to heed the images of God that
live in us. If we hold on long enough in the work of playing with those unconscious images alongside our conscious ones, and all of them next to the images of God
given us in Scripture and tradition, then we may even
find ourselves moved by grace to reach beyond every
human source to the unknown source itself.

Psychologically this inversion of consciousness feels
like reaching through and beyond the inner gods of superego and ego-ideal, through the particular archetypes

that run through our own lives, to gather together every possible strand of the central indefinable self that we know now as our core of being. And what have we reached? What but the great vast dark unknown mystery that belies all our fixed categories of thought and our confident sense of apprehending it. Our knowing has been transformed into an unknowing, an eager longing that changes everything about us, makes us a new shape and size at the core. No longer do ideas or symbols or specific images mediate the divine to us. We enter the precincts of immediate knowledge, where our own poor selves are the means through which we experience the immanent transcendent God.

II.

Some of the questions asked after the materials of the first three chapters were delivered as lectures sharply address the points I have been trying to make about the place of the psyche in the religious scheme of things. An important question is how the ego houses what belongs to it, and especially its own little evils, and, as a corollary, how might a church look that really took up this task.

To "house" means just that; it means not to suppress or repress or extinguish anything we are giving house room. It does not mean having one's psyche all tidied up, marched to order, everything understood. Those neatenings and straitenings reflect only an obsessive hygiene, a self- defeating urge to surface perfections. Housing means space, awareness, making room in consciousness for all the unknown presences that exist in us, between us, among us.

I often say to students that while we sit and talk, behind me looms an alligator, and behind you, a leopard, and over there a hyena.[10] Do we know about these astonishing presences? Chances are we do not. More likely, the other person over there will know before I do about my alligator or your leopard. They exist but we remain unconscious of them. To house them does not mean we must transform them into some little lizards in an aquarium on a living-room table. It means we must know that alligators and leopards and hyenas live with us, in our premises. Go to a zoo and look at an alligator. Look into its eyes. It does not look back at you; it has its own independent life that respects such independence. Housing means a management. There must be provision, a space where the alligator can go. You have to keep your eye on it, get to know its habits and what it likes to eat, whether it looks back at you or not. After a hundred years of analysis and other related forms of gaining self-knowledge, there one is with the same old alligator![11] Has anything changed? Yes, our knowledge of it, our awareness of its habits, our ability to protect our toes and those of other people from its bites. The achievement and the limitation, both, convict us of our finitude.

On an interpersonal level things get complicated. Spaces get crowded with one's own alligator, the other's leopard, the third one's hyena. They not only get crowded; they become dangerous. Our alligators may start nibbling on the fingers of our neighbors who may react violently, yelling at us, "Cut that out!" We say, "Cut what out?", oblivious but not innocent of what is going on. Nasty conflicts blow up. Translate this conversation into politics or labor disputes to see how serious this sort of thing can be. Take peace talks between warring nations as an example. Assume good faith on all sides. Everyone

sincerely wants improvement of communication, reduction of fear along with reduction of arms, and increase of
trust between the warring peoples. That is the conscious
intention, comfortably avowed by all. But unconsciously
the opposite state of affairs exists. We have a zoo full of
animals tearing at the bars to get at each other and
everyone who comes to stare at them. We do not see the
alligators, leopards, and hyenas of greed. We do not
recognize the hate and power-seeking as belonging to
ourselves. It always comes from others! So we are ready
to attack and fight. That way we can go on disowning the
alligators that belong to us and farm them out to the
enemy. We must withdraw such projections and claim our
own beasts if anything resembling peace is to break out,
in the small as well as the large conflict. That means
making conscious room for battalions of alligators, or
never breaking down the barriers between our consciously seeking agreement and our unconsciously refusing it.

See our own animals, see those that belong to others.
We need to notice that those others also have projections
onto us and we must remember that projections are not
mere phantasms. They can kill. Their alligators now, not
ours, may be biting at our feet, threatening us, leaving us
with no safe land to stand upon. Withdrawing our own
projections will help a great deal, but it is not a cure-all.
We must be aware that projections come from all sides so
that we may not be controlled by them, any of them, ours
or theirs or anyone's.

When contesting parties struggle to deal with their
projections a way is opened to see the differences that
remain between them even though both seek the same
goal, namely peace. Seeing the other this way aids understanding. For example, to study the literature of modern
Russia and its spirituality, however vestigial, will give us

a view from the ground up of what power and powerlessness mean from a Soviet point of view, what suffering means to the Russians, what such a people is willing to live and die for. The resultant perception must change our understanding of how to speak to the Soviets.[12]

Jung is a depth psychologist who wrestled his whole life with these matters. It is amazing that a twentieth-century analyst should take up the issue of the Trinity or the Mass or the problem of evil or the nature of God and with so much openness to the issues involved, ancient and modern. Still, if you insist on reading his *Answer to Job* as a metaphysical statement, serious problems arise. Jung himself advises us against taking his book that way, as an ontology. See it, he says, rather as his own subjective emotive confession.[13] It is important advice. One of the shifts we are undergoing as a result of depth psychology is away from easy security in intellectual constructs. Instead now we have a plethora of subjective confessions and wrestlings toward personal solution that we pool and share, sometimes profitably, sometimes not so well.

My understanding of Jung is that he finally did not know where to put the bad.[14] He could not get a net over it. But he could not and did not deny or repress it. He struggled with it. His personal life and his life with women show this struggle and even the nastiness that inhered in it. In his autobiography he writes obliquely of having done terrible things but that he could not help himself.[15] The unpublished parts of his book, apparently censored by his family, said a great deal more. What I think he was saying was: "I did not create myself this way. If I think it is all my fault I shall never be able to get out of bed again. So God must have something to do with it." That is where he put the bad—into and onto God. God, like Jung, struggled with evil and unconsciousness. God

needs Job's vociferous objection to the undeserved suffering inflicted upon him to call to God's conscious attention God's own evil side.[16]

For Jung this solution to his problem, masquerading as
Job's, worked. He could see then our efforts to struggle
consciously with our own shadow sides, with all the opposites in conflict within us, as our way of participating
in God's life and of carrying the incarnation onward. The
process of sanctification in Christianity, which brings
souls to blessedness, was consciously an acceptance of
this conflict with our evil shadow sides and God in fact
depends on us to do just this.

This attitude of Jung's holds some of the appeal that
the Zoroastrian religion holds: we can line up on the same
side with God, or Ahuramazda, and fight for the good
against the forces of darkness. For Jung, the saving good
was consciousness. God needs our consciousness. For
myself, I think that is simply where Jung projected his
particular struggle and particular God-image onto God.
God causes the bad because God is not sufficiently conscious—that is Jung's symbolic equation. That is where
the ladder of his images ended and the gap between him
and God was foreclosed. Openness was not allowed its
own space.[17]

When we look to the church and extend the task of
housing what belongs to us, we see a shift in the
psychological nature of that institution. Generally the
church has been identified with a superego function.
When the church is asked to do its work of housing, it is
its ego-function that dominates. The church has long had
to suffer identification as cultural superego in spite of all
the awkwardnesses of the term and its applications.
Freud's superego concept has survived in the basic
psychological vocabulary against gross distortions that

reduce the superego to nothing but a crabbed list of thou-shalt-nots, a moralizing apodictic set of prescriptions, particularly against any glad acceptance of aggression or sexuality. Such a reduction of the church is constricting and unprofitable, not to say false.

In defense of Freud it must be said he understood by the superego something that can be an immensely positive force in the psyche if it has developed its powers in primarily beneficent ways. A good working superego is like a fund of money in the bank. It is a rich resource of energy to draw upon when needed. It is a steady wind behind one's sail. This energy, these resources, feel natural and powerful when they are at full strength. Available and accessible, they make us feel possible. We have permission to do what we choose feels right to do. We have strong backing, so to speak, that garners community support, connects to others, and promotes our projects with others. We are not punished now but supported by our superego, not restricted but guided. The full weight of the collective system stands behind those individuals succeeding, not only for themselves but for all those with whom they share their lives.

When the church is associated with this sort of positive superego, it is experienced as life-giving. Here is a superego friendly to the ego without being wishy-washy, with an open attitude that accepts behavior rather than censures it. The superego does not stand apart in this guise either, wagging its finger at the ego. Instead, the superego instructs, inspires, encourages. Goodness knows we need that from the church! We need to hear from the church simply, clearly, that there is a God, that there is joy and life abundant. I would not want to see the church lose this extraordinary positive superego-function. Curiously, however, I think we cannot see it nor understand it unless we shift our attention to the church's ego-functions.

The church's ego-role is space-making, to offer a firm and big enough space that people trust enough to bring all of themselves into it—the bad, the troubled, the uncertain, the vengeful and resentful parts of themselves, and the eager, lively, glad and ambitious parts. All are invited to the banquet. Feeling thus housed and held in being, people can risk examining who they really are. They can go right into what makes them anxious. They can look at their murderous responses to other people, other congregations, other sects, other countries that both fascinate and frighten them. In the ego-role the church encourages awareness of what really goes on in our secret hearts, in our actual ways of living in our families, with our friends, at work, in society and parish, in every part of our world, in our actual experiences and beliefs about God. For a very large space is needed.

None of this is to make the church into a kind of collectivized ego with all its possibilities of tyranny and control. Rather, it is only to speak of the church, metaphorically, *as if* it participated in ego-functions. Again a gap intercedes. That *as if* figure of speech describes the ego as space-maker more than as master. For better or worse, the church is the place in Christendom where space is made for a shared consciousness of our roots in being. Here we may sort through the good and the bad. Here we may dare to confess where we were wrong. Here we may reach to gratitude. Here we may remember and circle round the good which announced itself in person, not as a perfect utopian good, but as a related one. Here we circle round all the joys of that contradictory but grace-filled world. Rilke's words might

be read as the church's:
    I am circling around God,
    around the ancient tower,
    and I have been circling for
    a thousand years
    and I still don't know if I am
    a falcon, or a storm,
    or a great song.[18]
When we think of the church as if it were a space of
ego-consciousness in Christendom, we include pre-ego
levels of life too. Indeed, this is all that such an ego-consciousness would be, open to impulses, instincts, to indefinable, irrational perceptions and apperceptions of
reality that are not yet differentiated into object and subject. This is a level of being which for centuries was recognized as an achievement of mystic consciousness. This
sturdy sort of space-making and housing conducted by
the church-ego brings a quality of listening to the
dialogue between persons speaking to and hearing each
other which supersedes the content of what is being said.
The church that houses all that comes into it, that houses
the gap between what we know and what can never be
known, contains both the archaic foundation of belief and
all that we now mean by "grace." This sort of church offers space for people to allow the unconscious to function, fostering that full sense of the other we call empathy
at the deepest level.[19] Such a church happily entertains
much silence in its services and is strong enough to face
much violence. To take just one example, this church
could face and try to make space for violence done to
women and to children, to know it and acknowledge its
sources so as to combat and overcome it.
    Whether such violence is on the increase or simply our
consciousness of it, it is too much with us. Any of it is too

much. From a psychological point of view, violence toward women and children presents us with a grim example of projection and sadism. To put it theoretically, the feminine modality of being is being literally equated with females. Males who cannot tolerate their own feminine side feel almost impossibly threatened. Such men may feel as if they were drowning in an ocean, or completely absorbed in women's thoughts, feelings, bodies, as the mass murderer Charles Manson said he did.[20] A patient once said to me, "Woman is like primeval ooze, a quicksand that will suck you down and then you're gone."

The violent male projects terrifying threat onto the female and then feels compelled to beat it out of her. Woman does not exist as a person in her own right for a man of this kind. She is equated with what he fears and fears all the more as he beats what he fears by beating her. She is absorbed in his fantasy just as he fears he will be absorbed and disappear in her. That is why consciousness of the feminine mode in oneself is so absolutely crucial— to relieve women of this assaulting terror and to make us see that we need to bring our dread of that mode of being into open consciousness where we can control how we relate to it.

Theoretically, children carry a different symbolic meaning, representing our dependence, our helplessness, our smallness, and vulnerability—all our creative possibilities for a living future. That is what is abused, beaten, molested, ridiculed by child-abusers. Their projections onto children, which may in fact be our projections, must be recalled into conscious responsibility. But we cannot wait until everyone recalls his or her projection. We need all kinds of social management to protect children—and women—from abuse, laws, ef-

fective treatment for abusers and abused, sanctuaries for
the most threatened and threatening.

Finally, a church functioning as space-maker can house
the gap we all know between our God-images and God.
It is not the place where the gap is overcome, though the
church points brick by brick to our hope in that promise.
Those of you who are clergy, who work in the trenches of
day-to-day church life, can give many examples of the
conflict, the sullenness, the sloth, the hate, the-not-being-
able-to-stay-awake-to-what-matters, that are everyday
common places in the church. The composer Stravinsky
was impressive on that score; he said when interviewed
by *The New York Times* in his late eighties: "I want to be
awake! awake!" Only God overcomes the gap, in bits and
pieces, in individual souls, communally. The church can
help us ready ourselves for grace, help us to spy it, to take
it when it comes, to use it. A lay person can tell us in a
moment whether a church space will help in the soul
tasks. It is a matter of atmosphere, a scent, a spirit in the
air, that tells us quickly whether the clergy are wrestling
with the same gap in themselves, struggling with the gap
between God-images and what is revealed in Scripture
and tradition and by what God may seem to be saying to
us today. From a psychological point of view, no separation exists among us at the unconscious level. We touch
each other in the depths of the unconscious and mix with
one another. So if the clergy are struggling with these issues, the congregation will feel the effects. It makes a
space for others to do it. We make spiritual contributions
to each other in this way, for good or for ill.

A church conscious that the unconscious exists would
allow silences, gaps in actual rituals, to see what might
surprise us. Good Friday services in particular, I think,
need a great deal more silence, many more of the great

empty spaces in which we can feel the impact of the emptiness that suffering opens like a yawning cavern beneath our feet. Attention should also be given in church to the weight of projections that fall upon the clergy, where a congregation unconsciously demands that the priest fit its needs for mother or father or surrogate-lover or wise-man or whipping-boy or good-sister or minister-ing-angel. For a congregation to feel its clergy struggling with the gap between God and its God-images not only makes spiritual space, but also an effective spiritual com-bat against the assault of projections. The best defense against people projecting onto us is to live our own reality to the full. That is the way we really show ourselves to others. What they may want or need us to be, or try to coerce us into being, then simply falls away. The dis-crepancy between the image of us they carry and who we really are collapses. That is where the gap saves us.

III.

A striking way to make clear the place of the psyche in things religious is to compare psychoanalysis with the earthworm. It aerates the soil—the matter of our psyche. The spirit, then, like the air, can circulate through it. To work with the psyche is to address the concrete, to face the immediate steps needed, for example, to solve a problem, or in any way to work upon it. To say to some-one facing fear, "Trust in providence!" may be wise ad-vice in the abstract, but it must feel like invoking judgment from on high to the persons in a concrete situa-tion. That is precisely what they cannot do because of fear that a dire answer must then result or that a happy one will fail to occur. Portentous religious words in such situations inevitably bring fear with them. Grace may also be made present this way but we cannot correspond to it without first trying to loosen up all those knotty clumps of fear, each of them, one by one. Working with our solid blocks of anxiety, trying to loosen them and trace down their origins, opens channels in us to receive the grace to correspond with grace. This is a way faith grows downward into us and takes root in our deepest weaknesses in our most hidden places. It is also the way the Holy Spirit comes burning in, as with the woman who prayed the Jesus prayer. The Holy Spirit "batters and breaks" our hearts as it receives us in our weakness.[21]

The question of the feminine mode of being and its recovery to consciousness is an example par excellence of the interweaving of psyche and soul. Psychologically it is necessary, even crucial, to ask about the feminine. Its neglect in our religious discourse as in all other kinds of discourse skews perception of every aspect of life. But we cannot just jump to it. Theologically we cannot import and impose symbols of the feminine. Symbols grow from the ground up, as Tillich has so eloquently told us.[22] Their life lies in connecting what is in our depths to the unseen reality to which symbols point. We cannot simply take a symbol and install it in the liturgy or doctrine. Such a use of symbol, which is being used then more like a sign, speaks only of consciousness to consciousness. It does not speak out of the unconscious and it fails to speak to it of a transcendent reality. The harder way characteristic of the feminine mode of being is to receive, to ponder, brood over, and gestate, to wait, to move and to be moved by the birth of the new. This is so hard because our need is greater than our perception. We want to hurry the process, to fix the imbalance of the masculine and feminine quickly. We fall into the danger of a brisk masculine solution to the problem of the missing feminine.

In contrast, the feminine mode gives us the wiles to live next to the gap, from which new symbols or refurbished old ones will emerge. But when they come, they are strange to us, full of ambiguity, with uneven edges, a crude power, an upsetting spirit. It is the feminine way then to hover over this gap, to house it in the communal church, felt now like a big empty pit deep in the midst of our life together, accepting that our powerful personal God-images do not neatly match those in Scripture or tradition, but rather belong next to them, the new with the old. Awareness of the differences among the symbols can go a long way to protect us from the inevitable temptation to idolatry, to take the old or new part we know and feel at ease with and make it substitute for the new whole whose dimensions we do not know or feel certain about.

Faith groups, denominations, schools of depth psychology, ideologues in both religion and psychology all fall into the same great error, forgetting the gap that always must exist between our vision of things and reality. When we act summarily to close that gap we find ourselves with a preacher who knows that only one way, his way, will lead to salvation. We get a faith group drawing the boundary lines around its sect, sharply delineating those on the inside who subscribe to the right theology from those on the outside who question, doubt, differ in any way. We get those with "correct" political views standing certain and full of contempt over those pernicious others who insist on asking questions and giving way to the uncertainty they feel.[23] We get the denominational wars of depth psychology between dif-

ferent schools of theory and procedure, each one claiming to have the whole truth and rejecting all others' angles
of vision, even the faintly heterodox in their own group.

A willingness to live with less clarity does not only
bring fuzziness and uncertainty; it also assures tolerance
of differences and acceptance of a wide range of varying
experiences. This is what the feminine mode of being as
a style of knowing and doing can bring. It can open us to
hear many confessions of many different kinds of experience of the meeting of psyche and spirit, even if we
do not yet have any clear constructs of the nature of
transcendent being. Feminine wiles allow us to know
things of profound importance without knowing anything for sure. We can be moved in this way to entertain
the radical notion that we, in our scruffy and magnificent
humanness, might make a fourth person to add to God's
three, to speak symbolically. We, all of us, could turn out
to be the feminine element in relation to the Godhead. For
all of us, men and women both, bring the concrete, down-
to-earth human containers, the matter, the ground in particular times, throughout history and up to today, in
which God takes up residence and manifests in the world.

The female aspect of divinity as a principle locates itself in the abyss of divinity, in the dark, the silence, out
of which Father, Son, and Spirit emerge.[24] The feminine
is the base of the pyramid formed by the three persons,
complementing but not absorbed into it. The essence of
the Trinity is affirmation and explication of the relationship central to being. It is the inspiriting source of all that
is, the defining element of all that is relationship
everywhere that there is relationship. The feminine
belongs to it as a ground of mysterious unknown depths,
the fruitful earth of Ruysbroeck, the great silence of Eckhart, the ground of being of Tillich. It is, as we must not

tire of saying, the containing Vièrge Ouverte who when she opens reveals the divine Trinity that she holds.

At this moment in the history of consciousness, the feminine appears not as principle in the abstract, but as a much needed mode of being in our particular lives. It is our special mode today to receive and incarnate and relate to the giant mystery of the divine as it is experienced by each of us in large and small lives. The feminine is the mode of consciousness that acknowledges this presence of the great mystery without identifying with it, that houses it without thinking it is only another way of speaking about ourselves, that we somehow are it. For those who see this and understand it and accept it, feminine metaphors abound. Such a style of consciousness holds and responds, mixes and differentiates the human from the divine as the mother gathers in and separates herself from her child; it receives and penetrates friends and guests and colleagues as a woman does her lover; it sees and does not see, takes in and puts aside as unavailable feelings, thoughts, and experiences as the wise old woman does and with her quiet authority; it mixes the old and the known with the new and unknown into something radically surprising as the wily witch does with her potions.

When we yield to this, the astounding possibility that we, every one of us, compose the feminine element in the Godhead, in the Trinity, we perform our greatest act of housing. We finish our burrowing as earthworms. We accept and revel in the fact that we provide the container in which the divine can take up residence and be born into the world, a container for a container, for that great tent of being that houses us, that pulls us in this containing of containers into the currents of its inner life of ceaseless love.

NOTES

1. Jung says two things that speak directly to the ego-self relation within an individual that affects and is affected by the individual's relation to the group. The self creates the group, but paradoxically the group can develop no farther than the individuals who comprise it.

   "... a positive relationship between the individual and society is essential, since no individual stands by himself but depends upon symbiosis with a group. The self, the very centre of an individual, is of a conglomerate nature. It is, as it were, a group. It is a collectivity in itself and therefore always, when it works most positively, creates a group. ..." C. G. Jung, *Letters*, Vol. I, p. 508.

   "... the value of a community depends on the spiritual and moral stature of the individuals composing it." (p. 30)

   "The fragile existence of the individual, the unique carrier of life. ..." (p. 39)

   "Without consciousness there would, practically speaking, be no world, for the world exists as such only in so far as it is consciously reflected and consciously expressed by a psyche. *Consciousness is a precondition of being.* ... The carrier of this consciousness is the individual ...." (pp. 46–47)

2. See, for example, Edward F. Edinger, *The Creation of Consciousness: Jung's Myth for Our Time* (Toronto: Inner City Books, 1984) and *The Bible and the Psyche: Individuation and the Old Testament* (Toronto: Inner City Books, 1986), See also Murray Stein, *Jung's Treatment of Christianity, The Psychotherapy of a Religious Tradition* (Wilmette: Chiron, 1986).

3. See Ann Belford Ulanov, "Needs, Wishes and Transcendence," in *Picturing God*.
4. See Phyllis Grosskurth, *Melanie Klein, Her World and Her Work* (New York: Alfred A. Knopf, 1986), Part 5, Chapters 1, 2, and 3.
5. See D. W. Winnicott, *The Spontaneous Gesture, Selected Letters of D. W. Winnicott*, ed. F. Robert Rodman (Cambridge: Harvard University Press, 1987). In a letter on pages 34–35 Winnicott expresses his urgent feeling to Melanie Klein about the importance of keeping psychoanalytic language alive and combatting its rigid formularization:

"I personally think that it is very important that your work should be restated by people discovering in their own way and presenting what they discover in their own language. It is only in this way that the language will be kept alive. If you make the stipulation that in future only your language shall be used for the statement of other peoples' discoveries then the language becomes a dead language, as it has already become in the Society. You would be surprised at the sighs and groans that accompany every restatement of the internal object clichés by what I am going to call Kleinians. . . .

". . . Your ideas will only live in so far as they are rediscovered and reformulated by original people in the psychoanalytical movement and outside it. . . . You are the only one who can destroy this language called the Kleinian doctrine and Kleinism and all that with a constructive aim. If you do not destroy it then this artificially integrated phenomenon must be attacked destructively. It invites attack . . . ."

6. See Ann Belford Ulanov, "On the Christian Fear of the Psyche," in *Picturing God*.

7. See, for example, Don Browning, *Religious Thought and the Modern Psychologies* (Philadelphia: Fortress Press, 1987). The author intends, he says, to examine the ethical and metaphysical horizons of depth psychology, but he neglects the literature of the unconscious and religion. He analyzes upwards, so to speak, into conscious categories of symbol systems and definitions of the good, while leaving out the amazing fact and experience of the unconscious, within us and among us, a fact and an experience that challenge all our tidy systems.

8. See Ann Belford Ulanov, "Picturing God," in *Picturing God*, pp. 168–169.

9. See, for example, Browning, *op. cit.*, pp. 237–238, for another example of the same kind noted above in footnote 7.

10. These beasts are likely symbols for what Jung calls our shadow—those parts of ourselves that personify what we fear and would like to disown. They present the dark otherness of the unconscious symbolized by animals and reptiles who possess an autonomous life of their own out of the mystery with which they confront us and puzzle us and instruct us. See C. G. Jung, *Aion, Collected Works* 9:11, trans. R.F.C. Hull (New York: Pantheon, 1959), pp. 8–11.

11. Masud Khan writes, "I make a distinction between *self-knowledge* and that self-consciousness, which is insatiably fed by introspection (privately), and often by free-association in analysis. . . . It is only when a patient can begin to use insight to *know* himself that he can begin to have a *new outlook* on his life." M. Masud R. Khan, "Fate-Neurosis, False Self and Destiny," in *Winnicott Studies, The Journal of the Squiggle Foundation*, London, I, Spring 1985, p. 13.

12. This idea of requiring diplomats to know Russian language and culture and to read Russian literature, history, and spirituality as a way of preparing adequately for such political jobs originates with my husband, Barry Ulanov.

   Petru Dumitriou holds a similar view. In a presentation at Union Theological Seminary in New York City in 1984, he described the Russian understanding of government as utterly different from ours. He said something like this: to people who for three hundred years government has meant brutal, total power—of Mongol hordes sweeping down from the north, pillaging villages, carrying off young people, crops, animals, then a government of despotic czars, and now the Politburo, to such a people the Western notion of participating in government is meaningless. See Petru Dumitriou, *To An Unknown God*, trans. James Kirkup (New York: Seabury Press, 1982).

13. C. G. Jung, *Answer to Job* in *Psychology and Religion: West and East, Collected Works* 11, p. 365, para. 361.

14. Here I am thinking of Melanie Klein's theory of reaching the depressive position psychologically. By this she means we see, feel, and suffer the facts of bad, of hostile, of downright evil emotions, impulses, and wishes both in ourselves toward those we love and admire and of similar response in those whom we love directed toward ourselves. For a specific example, see Melanie Klein, *Narrative of a Child Analysis* (New York: Delacorte Press/Seymour Lawrence, 1961), pp. 75–76.

15. See C. G. Jung, *Memories, Dreams, Reflections*, ed. Aniela Jaffé (New York: Pantheon, 1963):

   "The man, therefore, who, driven by his daimon, steps beyond the limits of the intermediary stage, truly enters the 'untrodden, untreadable regions,'

where there are no charted ways and no shelter
spreads a protecting roof over his head. There are no
precepts to guide him when he encounters an un-
foreseen situation—for example, a conflict of duties.
(p. 344)

"I have offended many people, for as soon as I saw
that they did not understand me, that was the end of
the matter so far as I was concerned. I had to move on.
I had no patience with people—aside from my
patients. I had to obey an inner law which was im-
posed on me and left me no freedom of choice. . . .

"For some people I was continually present and
close to them so long as they were related to my inner
world; but then it might happen that I was no longer
with them, because there was nothing left which
would link me to them. I had to learn painfully that
people continued to exist even when they had nothing
more to say to me. . . . In this way I made many
enemies. A creative person has little power over his
own life. He is not free. He is captive and driven by
his daimon. . . .

"This lack of freedom has been a great sorrow to me.
. . . I am fond of you, indeed I love you, but I cannot
stay. There is something heart-rending about that.
And I myself am the victim; I *cannot* stay. But the
daimon manages things so that one comes through,
and blessed inconsistency sees to it that in flagrant
contrast to my 'disloyalty' I can keep faith in un-
suspected measure." (pp. 356–357)

16. See C. G. Jung, *Answer to Job*, in *Psychology and Reli-
    gion: West and East, Collected Works* 11, pp. 373, 404,
    paragraphs 575, 639. See also C. G. Jung, *Letters*, Vol.
    2, p. 436.

17. A different view of evil is suggested in Ann and Barry

Ulanov, *Religion and the Unconscious*, pp. 39–41. The fact of evil destroys any image we project onto God. The fact of evil places God well out of our control, altogether different from and beyond our wishes for protection and solace: "Evil in its various forms so defies our wishes, defeats our projections, and dismays our fantasies of a good and loving world where we will all be well and happy, that many people feel their projected image of God cannot survive the inevitable destruction of such an image. Their faith founders at precisely this point. Their image of God as good dies because evil flourishes. They do not notice that God survives this destruction. . . . Those who do notice endure an extraordinary evolution in their religious sensibilities. They see that God is really 'other,' more so than they had risked perceiving before, and that evil is really a mystery, not a problem to be solved with childish wishes that everyone will somehow do the right thing. The profundity of sin throws into bold relief the transcendent otherness of a God even the goodness of whom cannot be simply identified with human conceptions of goodness. Our projections onto God shift to become means of perception, clues to God's existence. . . . Projections lead us far, to the edge of what we can perceive. They take on a salutary function, bowing before what exists on the other side. They point to it. They no longer define it."

Any thinker can be usefully studied just at the point where the thinker's projections are evident. For that is the edge of his or her knowledge pushing out into the dark unknown. The reader usually catches some sense of where this point, or frontier, exists for such authors. Their arguments seem overdetermined; they repeat their views more than several times, thus conveying an emotional insistence that their view must be accepted. Just there, the reader can see the gap between the authors' vast knowledge and the even more vast unknown they are trying to capture in the net of their theories.

18. *Selected Poems of Rainer Maria Rilke*, trans. Robert Bly (New York: Harper & Row, 1981), p. 13. The poem is taken from number 2 of Rilke's *A Book for the Hours of Prayer*.

19. Empathy, Heinz Kohut tells us, is one of the means (and results) of the transformations of narcissism. A disordered narcissism leaves us wounded, feeling unseen, unreflected, uncherished. Such a wound compels us to seek others' attention, constantly positioning ourselves in the limelight, using others only to reflect or to gratify needs and wishes of our own. The healing of such a wound means filling in that damaged place with newly grown capacities to maintain self-esteem and values and goals that hold our enthusiastic attention. Transformation of narcissism depends on another's empathic attention and results in our capacity to give such careful attention to others.

Transformation goes still further, however. Narcissism constellates the religious issue of being seen as a unique creation of God, making a creature capable of relation to deity. A person suffering from disordered narcissism falls into identification with this transcendent energy, in Jung's language, with the self. The self needs the ego to turn around and see it and be seen by it. When we fall into identification with this energy, we are driven, sometimes ruthlessly, to pursue others' attention to us, arrogating to ourselves the central place of the self. What is needed is metanoia, a turning around and seeing this self that wants to be seen and that sees our little ego. It is a step forward, into clarity, not back into disorder. In religious language, this transformation means to worship God, not some ego-need.

We could say that a narcissistic disorder concerns an ego-self disorder, rather than instinctual problems or a breakdown in ego defense. Narcissism might be described as dealing with the mystery of identity through a disorder of incarnation.

For reference see Heinz Kohut, *How Does Analysis Cure?*, chapter 9; see also, C. G. Jung, "Introduction to the Religious and Psychological Problems of Alchemy," in *Psychology and Alchemy, Collected Works*, Vol. 12, trans. R.F.C. Hull (New York: Pantheon, 1953); see also Nathan Schwartz-Salant, *Narcissism and Character Transformation* (Toronto: Inner City Books, 1982).

20. "We live in a woman's thought, this world is hers. But men were meant to be above, on top of women. . . . I am a mechanical boy, I am my mother's boy. . . ." Ed Sanders, *The Family*, p. 142, cited by Bradley A. TePaske in *Rape and Ritual: A Psychological Study* (Toronto: Inner City Books, 1982), p. 59. See also R. C. Zaehner, "The Reality of Wickedness," *The City Within the Heart*, pp. 36–44.

21. André Louf, "Humility and Obedience in Monastic Tradition," in *Cistercian Studies*, Volume XVIII, 1983:4, p. 271.

22. See Paul Tillich, "The Religious Symbol," *Daedalus, Journal of the American Academy of Arts and Sciences*, 87, 3, 1958; see also Ann Belford Ulanov, *The Feminine in Christian Theology and in Jungian Psychology*, chapter 5,

"The Symbol and Theology."

23. See Ann Belford Ulanov, "Picturing God," in *Picturing God*, pp. 170–171.
24. See Ewert H. Cousins, *Male-Female Aspects of the Trinity in Christian Mysticism*, Kristine Mann Library, C. G. Jung Institute, New York City.